RESOURCE BOOKS FOR TEACHERS

series editor
ALAN MALEY

DICTIONARIES
JON WRIGHT

Oxford University Press

OXFORD

UNIVERSITY PRESS

Great Clarendon Street, Oxford OX2 6DP

Oxford University Press is a department of the University of Oxford.
It furthers the University's objective of excellence in research, scholarship,
and education by publishing worldwide in

Oxford New York

Auckland Bangkok Buenos Aires Cape Town Chennai
Dar es Salaam Delhi Hong Kong Istanbul Karachi Kolkata
Kuala Lumpur Madrid Melbourne Mexico City Mumbai
Nairobi São Paulo Shanghai Taipei Tokyo Toronto

OXFORD and OXFORD ENGLISH are registered trade marks of
Oxford University Press in the UK and in certain other countries

ISBN 0 19 437219 7

Typeset by Oxford University Press

Printed in China

Acknowledgements

Published books often bear little resemblance to the ideas they start as. The activities in this book have been tried, tested, reshaped, and reformulated many times over a number of months and, in some cases, years. This would not have been possible without a great deal of help from many others. I am very grateful for the ideas and input of many teachers and students, in particular my colleagues Val Hennessy, Nick Regan, and Bec Wallis at The Language Project, and there should be a special mention for Etsuko Mizuno, too.

I am very grateful for the work of the team at OUP who have provided guidance, help, and support in addition to a lot of very close reading and acute comment throughout the process of turning a collection of ideas and activities into the book you are reading now. I must also thank the anonymous readers for their comments on earlier drafts of the book.

The faults that remain are, of course, mine.

The author and publisher are grateful to the following for permission to use extracts and adaptations of copyright material:

David Cheal for 'Reviews: Great Depression', reproduced with the permission of the author. This article originally appeared in the *Daily Telegraph*.

The *Daily Mail* for 'Constable picture wins the Turner (no, not that Constable)' by Kate Ginn and Terri Judd, 'Captain Cool fights off attacker to land jumbo', and 'On a wing and a prayer, the making of an in-flight movie' by June Southworth © *Daily Mail*.

Financial Times Syndication for permission to reproduce 'Dune-hopping through the sands of Africa' by Jack Barker, *Financial Times* 22 November 1997.

Oxford University Press for extracts from the *Oxford Wordpower Dictionary* © Oxford University Press, 1993.

Prentice Hall Europe for permission to adapt an extract from *Dictionaries, Lexicography and Language Learning* edited by Robert Ilson. Copyright © 1985 Pergamon Press Ltd. and the British Council.

Telegraph Group Limited, London, for 'Cities supply the bear essentials' by John Hiscock © 1997.

Although every effort has been made to trace and contact copyright holders before publication, this has not always been possible. We apologize for any apparent infringement of copyright and if notified, the publisher will be pleased to rectify any errors or omissions at the earliest opportunity.

Contents

The author and series editor

Jon Wright is co-founder and Director of Studies of The Language Project, Bristol, a small school with a special focus on teacher training and developing innovative learner-centred materials. He taught in schools and universities in France, Germany, and the UK before starting The Language Project, and has given presentations and led teacher training seminars in a number of countries. He has many years' experience as an examiner, and has written and reviewed for various EFL publications over the years, which has included work as Reviews Editor for the *EL Gazette*. He worked with Dave Willis on *Basic Grammar* for Cobuild, and current projects include materials that help learners learn idiomatic English, and new ways of teaching grammar and vocabulary.

Alan Maley worked for The British Council from 1962 to 1988, serving as English Language Officer in Yugoslavia, Ghana, Italy, France, and China, and as Regional Representative in South India (Madras). From 1988 to 1993 he was Director-General of the Bell Educational Trust, Cambridge. From 1993 to 1998 he was Senior Fellow in the Department of English Language and Literature of the National University of Singapore. He is currently a freelance consultant and Director of the graduate English programme at Assumption University, Bangkok. Among his publications are *Literature*, in this series, *Beyond Words*, *Sounds Interesting*, *Sounds Intriguing*, *Words*, *Variations on a Theme*, and *Drama Techniques in Language Learning* (all with Alan Duff), *The Mind's Eye* (with Françoise Grellet and Alan Duff), *Learning to Listen* and *Poem into Poem* (with Sandra Moulding), and *Short and Sweet*. He is also Series Editor for the Oxford Supplementary Skills series.

Foreword

Dictionaries, whether bilingual or monolingual, have long been part of the language learner's essential equipment. They are regarded by many as the repository of final linguistic authority, a bank account of words and meanings to be drawn upon in moments of need. The new generation of dictionaries, based on authentic samples of the language and computer corpora, offers both more information about the behaviour of words and more reliable information. This fact potentially enhances the importance of dictionaries for learners.

The sad fact remains however that, despite all the wealth of information dictionaries contain, the single most frequent use students make of them is to look up word meanings. Yet students' written work is often characterized by inappropriate word choice, lack of lexical precision, and unawareness of collocational constraints.

This resource book of dictionary activities has two main objectives:

In the first place it aims to improve and extend the ways in which students use the dictionary resource. It does this through extensive familiarization activities, as well as a wide range of activities focusing on all aspects of meaning, including collocations, idioms, and lexical sets.

Secondly, it sets out to show that, in the hands of a skilful teacher, the dictionary can become a resource for generating new and motivating communicative activities. From this perspective, the dictionary becomes the starting point for interactive discussion, game-like activities, competitions, and writing—activities which go well beyond the dictionary itself.

The first objective aims to turn learners into more effective dictionary users. The second aims to help teachers exploit the pedagogical resources offered by the dictionary, in order to promote learning.

The book will be welcomed for the important contribution it makes to opening up the dictionary to a full and rewarding range of uses.

Alan Maley

Introduction

The aims of this book

The two main aims of the book are:

1 to provide teachers with activities for improving dictionary-using skills;
2 to use dictionaries as a rich and varied resource for communicative activities.

Students benefit enormously from having the confidence and ability to use dictionaries properly. First of all, this skill enables students to solve their own language problems—after all, you cannot always be with them to help when things go wrong, or when new words crop up. As they become more familiar with the resources of the dictionary they use, and know where to find the answer to problems they have, they will be able to produce better English. But knowing how to speak English and knowing the words in the dictionary—even the unlikely case of knowing *all* the words in the dictionary—are not necessarily the same thing. The words do not mean very much unless they are used together to express some sort of communicable idea; knowing the words in the dictionary is essentially knowing *about* English, which is why many of the activities in this book involve communicating with or about what has been found in the dictionary.

Dictionary training

Dictionaries are among the most readily available, widely used, and cheapest learning resources that find their way into the classroom. They are also among the most difficult to use. We often think of dictionaries as just another book to help students learn, and overlook the fact that we need a wholly different set of reading skills to be efficient dictionary-users. It is surprising how little dictionary training goes on. Indeed, the whole idea of 'dictionary training' is relatively new.

There are a number of predictable problems that students face with dictionaries:

1 Students do not know which dictionary, or even which type of dictionary, to choose

Dictionaries are not all the same; size does make a difference. There are occasions when a pocket bilingual dictionary will do the job—looking up the names of common fruit in a market, for example—and there are others, perhaps more numerous, when it won't.

2 Finding the right word in the dictionary is not always straightforward

Where will you look for *unforgivably*? In most dictionaries it is not listed in its own right, so do you look for *unforgivable, unforgive, forgivable*, or *forgive*? How can a student know? And what about idiomatic expressions like *it's as easy as falling off a log*? Would you expect to find it in the entry for *easy*, or *fall, fall off*, or *log*? Which of the 20 or more meanings of *set* is the right one in a given context?

3 Understanding the information given about the word or expression you have looked up can be a problem

Once you've found the right **entry**, but before you reach the definition, you have grammatical and phonological information with special **codes** and symbols, which can be like another language and which may vary from one dictionary to another. A word with many meanings is likely to have several different codes—look at *set* in your dictionary again.

4 Finally, there are the often related problems of remembering what you looked up and being able to use it yourself

Often referring to the dictionary brings temporary enlightenment, but more than one meaning is frequently given for the same word. Sometimes learners hesitate about using the word themselves, or simply forget it once the dictionary is shut.

So perhaps it should not surprise us that many students prefer to turn to the teacher—that traditional 'walking dictionary'—for help and guidance instead. This is a pity in many ways, particularly for the student, because a major part of becoming an independent learner is learning how to use a dictionary with confidence. Helping your students become proficient dictionary users will give them greater control over their own learning.

Dictionaries as a teaching resource

Dictionaries are a teaching resource. They can serve as a focus for communication and classroom interaction, and a means of exploring personal preferences in learning styles. They naturally generate a great deal of thinking about meaning. There is no reason why dictionary activities should not be used as a basis for discussion, debate, role-play, or many other language activities. Instead of just referring *back* to dictionaries to solve problems of meaning encountered in texts or listening comprehension exercises, we can make the dictionary itself a primary source of interaction. Instead of being a book consulted in private, or largely for individual learning problems, it can become a springboard to all sorts of other communicative activities. By exploiting dictionaries as a source of interaction, we can help students develop their confidence as dictionary users, and an important spin-off is that students are exposed to a great deal of language data that will help them experience and explore the language as a system.

Teachers benefit as students develop better dictionary skills. Dictionaries provide an extra source of information in the classroom and add variety to lessons. They can provide useful support—not simply when you are in doubt about something but when you want students to confirm their own suppositions about an aspect of English. While students are working with dictionaries their focus is on learning, not on you, which allows you more time to provide individual guidance and support.

The activities in this book can be used with any learner's dictionary. It is important that your students use a dictionary which is suitable for their level—beginners will only be frustrated if they try to make sense of an advanced learner's dictionary; similarly, advanced learners will not derive great benefit from working with an elementary dictionary. In most cases, it does not matter if the students are using different editions, because there are valuable insights to be gained from comparing and contrasting different dictionaries. Where class sets of dictionaries are required, this is stated in the instructions.

Recent advances in dictionaries

Just as approaches to teaching grammar have changed over the years, so have dictionaries. One of the most significant changes in both domains has been the move from prescription to description. Until comparatively recently, lexicographers had to rely on their intuitive feelings about meanings and usage when producing dictionaries. Now computers hold vast corpora of written and spoken English compiled from very varied sources.

These have millions of words drawn from many contexts, formal and informal, literary and colloquial, covering a wealth of sources such as newspapers, film and television, instruction manuals, packaging, popular literature, and more. By examining these databases it is possible to establish evidence about the frequency of words in certain patterns. You can ask a database to print out all the instances of the word *hand*, for example, to see whether the noun is more common than the verb, how frequent the phrase *on the other hand* is, and which words it appears with most frequently: for example, *hand in, hand over, hand out, hand back, hand down*.

These 'concordances' give detailed pictures about common word partnerships in actual use, and insights gained from such analysis have now become an important source of information in dictionaries. Words with multiple meanings now generally list the statistically most common meaning first; examples given are generally authentic and are no longer made up. In other words, most dictionaries now do a much better job of describing English as it is actually used, so students have never had such a powerful tool to help them learn real English.

Different types of dictionary

There are many different types of dictionaries and one of the first choices learners make when they start learning a new language is which dictionary to buy. Not surprisingly, accessibility, cost and size are important factors. There are many arguments in favour of small bilingual dictionaries—they are generally cheap, they offer the support of translation into the mother tongue, and they are readily available. They can also be a cause of confusion, as demands of space result in drastic simplification. It is quite common for even large bilingual dictionaries to give a list of possible translations for verbs such as *go, take,* or *make,* with little information about which meaning applies in which context. Or perhaps they suggest a single translation, which can be even more misleading. Sometimes there is no guidance about the pronunciation of the word, or the grammatical patterns it operates in, and idiomatic expressions may not feature at all.

At the other end of the scale is the monolingual dictionary designed for native speakers; these can be vast, authoritative tomes which reflect the history and culture of the language, with information about when and where each word was first coined, its etymology, examples of use in literature, and so on. They are usually works of great scholarship which set out to be definitive works of reference, often including many thousands of words and their variants no longer in current use. This, when combined with their size and cost, generally means that they are not the most appropriate choice for foreign learners of English.

Between these two extremes are the monolingual dictionaries for foreign students, often called learner's dictionaries, which teachers often prefer students to use. These are often aimed at a specific language level and may also target specific age groups: there are children's and junior dictionaries for younger learners, elementary dictionaries, and dictionaries aimed at intermediate and advanced learners. The most important differences are in the number of words they set out to explain and define—the **headwords**—which can range from a few thousand for beginners to 80–100, 000 words and expressions in the case of advanced learner's dictionaries. In addition, the language of the definitions and explanations is tailored to the level of the learners. All good dictionaries use a much reduced **defining vocabulary** so that when students look up words, the language of the explanation itself is as simple and transparent as possible. Dictionaries at lower levels naturally tend to have more illustrations and the presentation of the grammatical information is simpler.

Another sort of learner's dictionary is the specialist dictionary aimed at professionals or students with a strong interest in a professional field such as medicine or business, where the focus is on key terms too specific for general learner's dictionaries. There are also dictionaries where words are categorized by topic—one version is the popular pictorial or visual dictionary.

The electronic dictionary is becoming increasingly popular. The hand-held versions offer many of the advantages of modern technology—they contain a great deal of information, can make use of sound, and can perform searches and other scanning operations much faster than we can turn pages. More powerful versions are the dictionaries on CD-ROM which are becoming a standard feature of many institutions, and which will doubtless become increasingly popular as they develop their full potential.

For the purposes of this book the focus is the learner's dictionary, the traditional paper dictionary. The main reasons for this are that it is still by far the most common and is likely to continue to be so for many years. Its size makes it easier for pairs and groups to work from a single copy. Electronic dictionaries do not offer the same opportunities to practise the reading skills that are a feature of many of the activities in this book; nor can the user easily make comparisons and associations between words in the same manner.

The purpose of the activities in this book is to help develop skills which will help learners with all types of dictionaries. The confidence that comes from becoming an efficient learner will help in all areas of language learning and production.

Features of dictionaries

Dictionaries for learners do far more than simply provide the meaning of a word—there are often study pages with handy notes about common problems; many have lists of irregular verbs, common first names, maps, and information about letter-writing conventions; and there are cross-references to related words or common opposites, for example. Each dictionary is different and it is important for the learners who use a dictionary to find out what is in it, what it means, and how to use that information.

Dictionaries and communicative teaching

In some ways it seems that dictionaries have been bypassed by the communicative methodologies that have dominated language classes in recent years. There are comparatively few activities designed for groups using dictionaries together; often we feel that when students reach for the dictionary to check a word, they are somehow interrupting the flow of the lesson.

Perhaps one reason for this is that we are vague about the role and status of the dictionary in the communicative classroom. Current thinking about language learning encourages risk-taking and all sorts of guesswork, with the aim of helping students to develop communicative strategies to overcome language problems; hypothesis formulation is seen as the basis of much learning, and experience either confirms students' hypotheses or encourages them to formulate a new hypothesis in the light of what they have discovered. Being unsure, having options, even being 'wrong' is accepted as a natural part of the learning process. With dictionaries, however, we tend to expect right answers, exact meanings, correct spelling and pronunciation, and there is no scope for error. This perhaps makes them appear rather intimidating and authoritarian.

At this point you may like to think about your own position regarding dictionaries and their role in your classes. Here are some questions to guide your thinking:

Practical points

1   Do you have a class set of dictionaries?
2   Do you have a favourite dictionary? If so, which one and why?

Teaching tactics

3 How often do you ask students to use dictionaries in class? At what stage of the lesson?

4 Do your students ever work together using dictionaries in class?

5 Is there any sort of lesson when you do not make use of the dictionary—grammar, listening, vocabulary, speaking, coursebook classes, etc? Why?

6 What sort of information do you ask students to check: spelling, grammar, pronunciation ?

7 Do you allow the use of bilingual dictionaries in class?

Dictionary training

8 How do you help students overcome the perceived problems of dictionary use?

9 How often do you refer students to a dictionary when they ask questions about grammar, spelling, pronunciation, etc.?

10 How important is it to study the example sentences when checking a word, and why?

Opinion

11 To what extent can using dictionaries be an enjoyable element of the class?

12 Would you ever discourage a student from using a dictionary in or outside the class, and if so, why?

13 To what extent do you think using an English–English learner's dictionary helps students to think in English?

14 Do you think bilingual dictionaries are more helpful to students when doing reading or writing work, and why?

Implications

Practical points: Regular access to a dictionary is absolutely essential for dictionary training and to encourage good dictionary habits. Only up-to-date dictionaries can teach up-to-date English. Do your class dictionaries have idiomatic expressions and the latest computer terminology? If you have a favourite dictionary, would you recommend it to your learners? Their level may be very different to yours, and their learning purposes and preferences may be different too.

In situations where class sets of dictionaries are not available, it is important for teachers and learners to be aware of the significant differences between different dictionaries.

Teaching tactics: Learners benefit from an approach which regularly involves dictionary use in small doses: 'little and often' rather than one monster session per month. But if dictionaries are only used in certain types of lessons, learners may pick up confused messages, such as that dictionaries cannot help with grammar problems or are only useful for learning new words. We should guard against this. Dictionaries can be a source of confirmation and a source of answers about new language items. If dictionaries are only used at the end of an activity, students may get the impression that dictionaries cannot be used as a stimulus.

Some teachers have 'rules' which restrict rather than encourage dictionary use. The issue of bilingual dictionaries divides teachers—some argue that it will not help with the learning and assimilation of English; others feel that recourse to translation and bilingual dictionaries is the most natural method of learning a foreign language, so why forbid it?

Dictionary training: Students do need training and guidance with dictionaries. Frequent use provides opportunities for learning, but does not itself guarantee that students will automatically learn the various codes and understand how to get more out of their dictionaries. There is also a big difference between looking up a word, checking a spelling, and studying an entry.

Opinion: Learners know that dictionaries are useful. Few, however, go as far as expecting to enjoy the process of consulting dictionaries. But learners will use dictionaries more readily and more profitably when they are taking part in an engaging activity. Enjoyable activities can have a positive impact on learners' retention of the language items learnt. This will help students to want to think in English—but there will of course be times when they can't. Bilingual dictionaries may prove the most useful on such occasions.

How to use this book

The activities are divided into the following six sections.

1 Getting started

This section contains activities to assess the current practice of the learners, and to diagnose problems with or reservations about dictionary use. It introduces the basic terminology and key features of a dictionary and has a number of activities that provide practice with the **alphabet** and spelling. These activities should be used at the start of a programme to ensure that students have the skills in place to learn more efficiently as time goes on.

2 Working with headwords

Practical problems of understanding the **codes** and finding the right word need to be dealt with before learners can feel comfortable with exploring the dictionary on their own; these are tackled in Chapter 2. The activities deal with finding the right word and the right **part of speech**, understanding **word formation**, and becoming familiar with the **phonemic symbols** used to give phonological information in dictionaries, so that students can make productive use of what they look up.

3 Working with meaning

Here the activities give a high priority to establishing and understanding relationships between words. In particular, students are encouraged to personalize their learning and make associations between words and senses, words and topics, and thus impose their own order on the purely alphabetical arrangement in dictionaries.

4 Vocabulary development

This section looks at ways of exploiting dictionaries to develop vocabulary. It contains activities on **lexical sets** (groups of words) and memory training tasks, and at the same time explores figurative uses of common nouns, and discovery learning of **idioms** and **collocations**.

5 Using texts

This chapter uses a variety of English texts, including authentic material, for language activities that focus to a great extent on integrated skills practice—not simply using dictionaries for comprehension work. Students explore texts and create their own, using dictionaries in the planning and checking stages of composition.

6 Bilingual dictionaries

The activities in this chapter focus on comparing the strengths and weaknesses of bilingual and monolingual dictionaries in different situations for both communicative and language learning tasks.

The Glossary (page 163) gives the meanings of terms which are important for dictionary use. Words in the book which are in **bold** (or ***bold italic*** in Activity headings) are explained in the Glossary.

The Index (page 169) helps you to find an activity on a particular topic quickly.

The Further Reading section (page 167) gives suggestions and comments on other useful books.

In general, the activities towards the beginning of each chapter introduce or review more basic features of dictionaries and dictionary use. As with so much else in language teaching, it is important to vary your approach and offer the class dictionary training in regular short sessions—little and often will ensure maximum interest and benefit. Of course, different classes will have different needs, so that it is likely that the activities will be used in different proportions according to the level, strengths, and interests of your class.

1 Getting started

The activities in this chapter are designed to familiarize students with the wealth of information that dictionaries can provide. The activities also introduce students to dictionary terminology (for example, 1.1, 'What's what?') and rehearse basic skills that will help them use the dictionary as effectively as possible, such as knowing where to look up a word (see 1.9, 'First things first', page 25). Anyone who opens the dictionary in the middle when looking for the meaning of 'yawn' is in for a long search (see 1.6, 'Lucky dip', page 21).

There are also activities to help you find out how students feel about using dictionaries and the problems that they face (1.4, 'Complete the sentence', page 19; and 1.7, 'Using, abusing, and overusing a dictionary', page 22). Later activities focus on spelling skills and familiarization with the alphabet, which can be a major hurdle for learners whose own language does not use the Roman alphabet.

In some activities, students may not actually need to refer to a dictionary. However, it is always a good idea to have a dictionary handy so that students get in the habit of checking when they are in doubt. Many of the basic skills practised here will be reviewed and developed in activities in other sections.

1.1 What's what?

LEVEL	**All**
TIME	**15–20 minutes**
AIMS	**To introduce or revise the basic layout and terminology of dictionary pages.**
MATERIALS	A copy of the 'What's what?' worksheet; a dictionary for each student.
PREPARATION	Make a copy of the worksheet for everyone, or make a similar worksheet using a dictionary at your learners' level.
PROCEDURE	1 Hand out the copies of the worksheet and ask the students to complete the task individually.
	2 Ask them to get into pairs and check their answers.
	3 Go through the answers, explaining any problems (see the end of the chapter (page 34) for an answer key).

WHAT'S WHAT?

A Look at the numbered parts of the page. Can you match the numbers to the corresponding letters ?

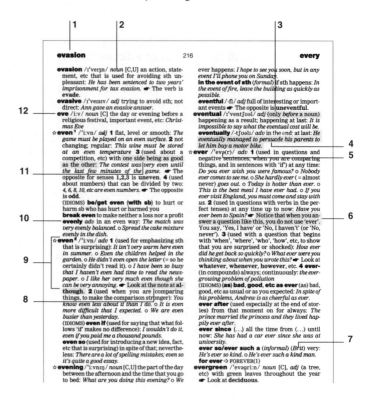

From the *Oxford Wordpower Dictionary*, p. 216

a Headword

b Grammar facts

c Phonemic transcription

d Definition

e Example

f Abbreviation

g Part of speech

h Usage notes

i Running head

j Cross-reference

k Entry

l Derivative

B Which piece of information from Task A tells you about:

1 the pronunciation of a word

2 the spelling of a word

3 other related words

4 how we actually use the word

5 what the word means

6 the first or last word on the page

7 what sort of word it is?

(Note: some of the questions have more than one possible answer.)

4 Ask the class to open their dictionaries to see if there are any differences from the examples on the worksheet. If so, what are they? If you are using different editions, make sure that the students know where to find the same information in the dictionaries they normally use.

COMMENTS   See the Glossary (page 163) for an explanation of dictionary terms.

1.2 What's in it?

LEVEL   **Elementary and above**

TIME   **30 minutes +**

AIMS   **To familiarize students with dictionary contents and dictionary terms; diagnosing problems; needs analysis.**

MATERIALS   A copy of the 'What's in it?' worksheet for each student and a dictionary for each pair.

PROCEDURE   1 Ask students in pairs to think of 5–10 features they will find in a dictionary, such as examples, definitions, or pictures. Allow a couple of minutes, prompting where necessary. They should not use a dictionary yet. Explain any new terms such as **usage notes** (see the Glossary, page 163).

2 Pairs compare notes in fours: can they name more than ten different features?

3 Distribute the worksheet and ask the students to complete it by checking in a dictionary. This will help them find their way around the dictionary.

4 Ask the groups to check their information with each other. If they have different dictionaries, this can expose important differences between publications. Make a note of any particular problems the class agree on and discuss how they can improve their confidence.

COMMENTS   1 Lower-level classes might prefer to do this in their own language.

2 Other activities in this book aim to address problems which may have been highlighted by this activity: the Index at the end of the book shows where to find activities on particular topics.

WHAT'S IN IT?

How easy is the information in your dictionary to understand and use?

Does it have the following features?

	Yes/no	Where?	1 = I need more help 5 = no problem
illustrations			1 2 3 4 5
examples			1 2 3 4 5
definitions			1 2 3 4 5
explanations			1 2 3 4 5
grammar information			1 2 3 4 5
pronunciation			1 2 3 4 5
synonyms			1 2 3 4 5
translations			1 2 3 4 5
list of irregular verbs			1 2 3 4 5
an introduction			1 2 3 4 5
idioms			1 2 3 4 5
details of register			1 2 3 4 5
usage notes			1 2 3 4 5
running heads			1 2 3 4 5
cultural information			1 2 3 4 5
other?			1 2 3 4 5

1. 3 What's important for you?

LEVEL	Intermediate
TIME	10 minutes +
AIMS	To think about priorities in using dictionaries and to teach dictionary terms.

MATERIALS   A copy of the 'What's important for you?' worksheet for each
                       student (optional).

PROCEDURE   1 Ask the students to think about why they use dictionaries. After
                         a few minutes, get them to compare their answers with their
                         neighbours.
                       2 Distribute the question sheet and ask them to complete it, or
                         write the questions on the board or overhead projector and ask
                         the students to copy it.
                       3 The students circulate to find the person who has the most
                         different answers to them. When they have found their
                         'partners', they should discuss why they have such differences.
                       4 Conduct quick feedback. Would anyone change their opinions?

WHAT'S IMPORTANT FOR YOU?

How important are the following for you when you use a
dictionary? Put them in order of importance from 1 to 12.

1 spellings   _____
2 grammar information   _____
3 pronunciation   _____
4 examples   _____
5 translations   _____
6 explanations   _____
7 meaning   _____
8 illustrations   _____
9 notes about similar words   _____
10 idioms   _____
11 understanding when and   _____
   how to use words
12 list of irregular verbs   _____

Photocopiable © Oxford University Press

1.4 Complete the sentence

LEVEL   **Elementary and above**

TIME   **20 minutes**

AIMS   **To assess how the learners feel about using dictionaries; to
                       diagnose problems, and check strategies.**

MATERIALS   A piece of paper for each student.

PROCEDURE 1 Tell the students to prepare for a dictation. Explain that you will dictate the beginning of a sentence, and that they must complete it themselves.

2 Dictate the following sentence beginnings:

  a I generally use dictionaries to …
  b I think dictionaries should …
  c One of the biggest problems I have with dictionaries is …
  d What I like about my dictionary is …

  Give the students two or three minutes to complete each sentence, individually.

3 Ask the students to circulate around the class comparing what they have written, and to find the person who has the most similar answers.

4 Each pair finds a pair with very contrasting answers. They discuss the reasons for their different answers.

5 What do the students find most useful? What do they need help with?

1.5 Look it up in a dictionary

LEVEL   All

TIME   10–15 minutes

AIMS   **To give students practice in formulating useful sentences when working with dictionaries; to give students practice in framing questions.**

PREPARATION   Make a copy of the 'Look it up in a dictionary' worksheet for each student.

PROCEDURE   1 Give out the worksheet and ask the students to complete it in pairs.

LOOK IT UP IN A DICTIONARY

Put the words in these sentences in the right order:

1 what word that mean does?
2 do you how it spell ?
3 pronounce it you do how ?
4 the difference X what and Y is between?
5 why up a look dictionary don't you in it?

Photocopiable © Oxford University Press

2 Go through the answers, making sure everyone can ask each question naturally, from memory. In pairs, the students ask each other the questions.

FOLLOW-UP

In pairs, the students look through the next unit of the coursebook, or through their vocabulary books, and think up two examples of each question from the worksheet. They form groups of four and test each other.

1.6 Lucky dip

LEVEL

All

TIME

5–10 minutes

AIMS

To help students get to the right part of the dictionary quickly; to raise awareness of the layout of the dictionary.

MATERIALS

A dictionary for each student.

PROCEDURE

1 Hold a dictionary up to the class with the pages facing the students. Ask them whereabouts the word *zoo* is, and ask them to help you open the dictionary at the right place. Now ask them to guess where the word *lucky* is. They should try to open their dictionary at that page. Count down 3–2–1 and then everybody opens their dictionary at once. Do not allow any page-turning.

2 Was anyone on the right page? How many people opened the dictionary at the letter L? How many people were further out than the letters I or Q?

3 Put the students in pairs and ask them what fantastic prize they would like to win in your lucky-dip competition. Encourage one-word answers, for example, *money, fame, holiday, car*. Explain that the prize can only be won by **one** person in each pair: the person who is closest to the key word. Now they try to open the dictionaries at the right page and see who the winner is.

FOLLOW-UP

With more advanced groups, you can develop the activity by explaining that they only win the prize if they open the dictionary at exactly the right page. If they fail, they must choose a *booby prize* from that page—something which is funny or slightly unpleasant perhaps, and write a paragraph to a friend about what they have won and how they feel.

1.7 Using, abusing, and overusing a dictionary

LEVEL	**Intermediate**
TIME	**25 minutes +**
AIMS	**To think about dictionary use; discussion.**
MATERIALS	A copy of the 'Dictionary advice' worksheet for everyone.
PROCEDURE	1 Give out the worksheet and ask students to work through it in pairs.
	2 Discuss the answers. What picture of dictionary use emerges?
COMMENTS	Questions 1 and 5 give an indication of how dependent on a dictionary the students are.
	Question 2 shows a rather limited view of dictionaries and may lead to many missed opportunities.
	Question 3 raises awareness of the vital differences (also explored in Chapter 6).
	Questions 4 and 9 are healthy learning strategies that help develop independence and memory training.
	Question 6 is a moot point: some words and phrases defy translation; being overdependent on translation often reduces fluency.
	Questions 7 and 8 are connected: many students find the act of writing an aid to memory, but it often helps to take personalized notes rather than simply copying what is in a dictionary. Including the context in which the word occurs in the class can help.
	Question 10 raises awareness of the wealth of grammatical information in dictionary entries.
	You may find it useful to check the Index (see page 169) for activities that can help with specific problems.
FOLLOW-UP	In groups of two to four, the students write advice about when to use dictionaries and how to use them wisely, based on the statements on the worksheet. These can be displayed as posters.

DICTIONARY ADVICE

Here are some things said by students about dictionaries.
Choose how much you agree or disagree: 1, 2, 3, 4, or 5? Why?
Circle your answers then compare them with a partner.

1 = disagree totally   *5 = agree totally*

1 It is impossible to use
   a dictionary too often.   1   2   3   4   5

2 You should use a dictionary
   only when reading.   1   2   3   4   5

3 Bilingual and monolingual
   dictionaries have the
   same information.   1   2   3   4   5

4 First guess the meaning,
   then look up a word.   1   2   3   4   5

5 Try to learn all the meanings
   of a word when you look it up.   1   2   3   4   5

6 It helps to translate every word
   you look up.   1   2   3   4   5

7 There's no point in copying
   information from a dictionary.   1   2   3   4   5

8 It's natural to forget what you
   read in a dictionary.   1   2   3   4   5

9 Always learn a word in a context. 1   2   3   4   5

10 If you need to learn grammar,
   get a grammar book.
   Dictionaries can't help.   1   2   3   4   5

1.8 The alphabet

LEVEL

Beginner to intermediate

TIME

30 minutes

AIMS

To improve familiarity with the alphabet.

MATERIALS

A copy of the 'Alphabet' worksheet for each student; a dictionary for each pair.

THE ALPHABET

A The English alphabet has 26 letters. Is that the same as your language?

B There are 5 vowel letters in English: o i a e u

Put the vowels in alphabetical order: 1.   2.   3.   4.   5.

C Quick quiz. How quickly can you answer these questions?

1 What is the letter before Z?

2 What is the letter after I?

3 Which letter comes after Q?

4 Which consonants come before and after E?

5 What are the two letters after U?

6 Which letter is missing in this sequence: F G H I K L M

7 Which letter is missing in this sequence: W U T S R Q

D Now write out the 26 letters of the alphabet in order:

_____

E Here are some familiar lists. Can you complete the words, then put them in alphabetical order?

1 M_nday, __esday, ___nesday, ___ rsday, __iday, __turday, __nday

2 _ an __ry, _eb_uary, __rch, _p__l, M __, __ ne, __ly , __g_st, ___tember, ___ober, __ember, ___ember

F Now write out in alphabetical order

1 Six different colours _____

_____

2 Ten different animals _____

_____

3 Ten different countries _____

_____

PROCEDURE

1 Give out a copy of the worksheet to each student, and ask them to work through it in pairs. They can check their answers in a dictionary.

2 Go through the answers for questions A–E (for a key see the end of the chapter, page 34).

3 For questions F 1, 2, and 3, ask one pair to read out their list. Tell the rest of the class to listen and write down any colours, animals, or countries they did not have. Then ask the class for any answers that have not been mentioned. Everybody writes down the new answers.

4 Give everyone two minutes to put *all* the answers into alphabetical order. When both members of a pair are absolutely sure they have every item, and in the correct alphabetical order, they put their hands up and read through their lists—which should now be identical to everyone else's. If they make a mistake, or miss out an item, the next pair has a go.

1.9 First things first

LEVEL

All

TIME

25 minutes

AIMS

To help students find words in word groups; to raise awareness about the presentation of *derivatives*, plurals, and *compounds* in dictionary entries.

MATERIALS

A copy of the 'First things first' worksheet for each student; a dictionary for each pair.

PROCEDURE

1 Give out the worksheet and ask the students to go through it, and then compare their answers in pairs.

2 Take feedback. If the class used different dictionaries, discuss the different results, if any.

COMMENTS

Generally dictionaries list compounds as entries in their own right, whereas irregular plurals and past tense forms are cross-referenced to the singular or infinitive form. Phrasal verbs tend to come before compound entries. Answers for sections B and C might vary. Generally, superlative, adverb, noun, and participle forms occur in the adjective or verb entries respectively. Idiomatic expressions are often listed under the first adjective, noun, or verb, sometimes with the exception of common verbs like *be* or *have*. For the answer key see the end of the chapter, page 34.

FIRST THINGS FIRST

A For each list decide which word appears first in the dictionary:

1	**a** mother	**b** moth	**c** mother-in-law
2	**a** cloth	**b** clothing	**c** clothes
3	**a** fisherman	**b** fish	**c** fishing
4	**a** first name	**b** first aid	**c** firstly
5	**a** feet	**b** foot	**c** football
6	**a** house	**b** housewife	**c** household
7	**a** country	**b** countryside	**c** county
8	**a** lightly	**b** light bulb	**c** light
9	**a** swam	**b** swimmer	**c** swimming pool
10	**a** take off	**b** took	**c** taker

B Do these words appear as headwords in your dictionary? If not, how can you find them?

1 happiest   2 explorer   3 dependable
4 theatrically   5 heard

Check in your dictionary.

C Which word would you look up to find the meanings of these idioms and expressions?

1 It's as easy as falling off a log.
2 He's as honest as the day is long.
3 Mind your own business.
4 Your jumper is back to front!
5 It was expensive but she bought it all the same.
6 You need eyes in the back of your head in this job!

Check in your dictionary.

1.10 Skimming and scanning skills

LEVEL

False beginners and above

TIME

5–15 minutes

AIMS

To provide scanning practice; to increase familiarity with dictionary terms.

MATERIALS

A dictionary for each pair; a copy of the 'Skimming and scanning' worksheet for each student.

PROCEDURE

1 Give out the worksheet and ask students to work in pairs. Explain any terms they do not understand.

2 Collect the completed worksheets and put them around the walls or on desks.

3 The students circulate to see which page looks the most interesting.

4 Allow a couple of minutes for the students to follow up their interest in any of the words or pages.

SKIMMING AND SCANNING

Open your dictionary at any page.
How quickly can you answer these questions?

On your page:

1 What are the first and last headwords?   _____

_____

2 Which is the longest headword?   _____

3 How many adjectives are there?   _____

4 How many headwords do you already know?   _____

5 Can you find a compound word?   _____

6 Is there an idiom? What is it, and what does it mean?   _____

_____

7 Which word has most different meanings?   _____

8 Can you find an irregular verb?   _____

9 Think of two topics you could talk about using headwords from this page:

a _____

b _____

Photocopiable © Oxford University Press

1.11 Alphabet game

LEVEL

Beginner to elementary

TIME

10–15 minutes

AIMS

To familiarize students with the *alphabet* and alphabetical order.

MATERIALS

A dictionary for each pair.

PREPARATION	Make a list of recent vocabulary (optional).
PROCEDURE	1 Either elicit or write on the board a list of vocabulary items recently dealt with in class. Jumble the words all over the board. 2 Explain that the students must copy the words down in alphabetical order as quickly as possible. If they like, it can be a race. 3 In pairs, they check their answers, consulting the dictionary if there are disagreements.
VARIATIONS	Other possibilities include asking the students to arrange the names of everyone in the class, or their favourite pop groups, or countries they have visited, in alphabetical order.
COMMENTS	You could specifically include words beginning with 'h', which is often omitted when students speak, or 'y', 'w', and other letters which many languages do not have.

1.12 Spelling activity

LEVEL	**Elementary and above**
TIME	**20 minutes**
AIMS	**To sensitize students to spelling problems.**
MATERIALS	A dictionary for each pair.
PREPARATION	Prepare a list of 10–15 words commonly misspelt in the class, perhaps from recent homework, or words you think they need to know how to spell for future work.
PROCEDURE	1 Ask everyone to take a piece of paper and divide it into two columns as follows:

Sure	Not sure

2 Tell them you are going to dictate some words, and they must write each word in one of the columns depending on whether they are sure how to spell it or not. They needn't worry if they don't know how to spell a word—they simply put it in the 'Not sure' column.

3 Dictate your list of words, giving each a number (the students should write the number too). Typical problems include:

accommodation	vegetable	teacher	woollen
separate	appearance	address	calendar
recommend	forgettable	island	chaos
language	foreign	necessary	catastrophe
yacht	Ireland	writing	whether
what	which	school	different
government	comfortable	stomach	believe

4 The students compare their answers in pairs. If they have two different versions of the same word in the 'sure' column, who is right?

5 The pairs check their answers in a dictionary.

VARIATION 1

You can introduce a competitive element by giving two points for each answer which is right in the 'sure' column, one point for each word in the 'not sure' column which is correctly spelt, and minus five for each wrong answer in the 'sure' column.

VARIATION 2

You can use this activity to present the key vocabulary of a text or topic you are going to study. When students are checking the spelling in step 5, make sure they also pay attention to the meaning of the new words, then ask them to guess what topic they are all connected to. When you give out the text, ask them to find and underline all the words dictated, then to check the meaning in that particular context.

Acknowledgements
I learnt this activity from a colleague, Val Hennessy.

1.13 Endless words

LEVEL

Beginner to intermediate

TIME

10–20 minutes

AIMS

To familiarize students with the *alphabet*; to help develop a feel for the shape of words and word *boundaries*.

MATERIALS

A dictionary for each pair.

PREPARATION

Make a list of new words you want the class to focus on.

PROCEDURE

1 Write on the board or overhead projector six words that are new to the class—but run them together with no breaks, like this:

nightbreakfastholidayhappytrafficpassport

2 Put the students in pairs and ask them to find the six words.

3 They check their answers in a dictionary.

4 Discuss (in their language, if appropriate) how they found the right answers. How did they know where one word ended and another began? Alternatively, go through the list, asking:
  – Can a word begin with these letters? (pointing at *ght*, *akf*, or *ayh*)
  – Can a word end with these letters? (pointing at *tb*, *oli*, *ytra*, or *icpa*)

FOLLOW-UP

Ask each pair to look through their vocabulary books, or to remember recent vocabulary items they have learnt, and to make a list of six words in the same way and pass it to their neighbours.

VARIATION

A slightly harder version is to incorporate one letter that does not belong in any of the words and ask the group to find it:

yachtdivisionsupermarketcbook (where **c** is the extra letter)

COMMENTS

This activity can be used to preview words that will come up in a reading or listening text to be studied later, or to revise vocabulary.

1.14 Spelling silent letters

LEVEL

Elementary to upper-intermediate

TIME

15 minutes

AIMS

To practise spelling words with silent letters; to encourage the use of the dictionary for spelling problems.

MATERIALS

A dictionary for each pair; a copy of the 'Spelling silent letters' worksheet for each student.

PROCEDURE

1 Hand out the worksheet. Explain that you are going to read out some words, each of which has a silent letter. The students try to fill in the gaps and spell the words correctly.

2 Read out the following words for intermediate level: *knowledge, receipt, psychology, sign, pneumonia, calm, muscle, thoroughly.*

  For elementary students, read: *comb, knife, autumn, foreign, castle, hour, Wednesday.*

3 The students compare their answers in pairs, then check in a dictionary.

4 Ask the students how they can take note of problems like silent letters when they are learning vocabulary. Possible solutions:
  – learn the **phonemic symbols**;
  – write the silent letters in another colour;
  – match the words by rhyme, for example, *comb—home*; *through—you.*

VARIATION

To provide more context, incorporate the words into a story. Read it out and ask the students to write down the words from the worksheet as they hear them.

SPELLING SILENT LETTERS

Intermediate

Listen to your teacher saying the following words, then try to fill in the missing letters. Be careful: each word has a silent letter.

1 _ _ o _ l e _ _ e	5 _ _ e u _ _ n i a
2 r e _ _ i _ t	6 c a _ _
3 _ s _ _ _ o l o _ _	7 m _ _ _ l e
4 s i _ _	8 t h o _ o _ _ _ l y

SPELLING SILENT LETTERS

Elementary

Listen to your teacher saying the following words, then try to fill in the missing letters. Be careful: each word has a silent letter.

1 c o _ _	5 c a _ _ _ e
2 _ _ i f e	6 _ _ u r
3 a _ t u _ _	7 W e _ _ _ _ d a y
4 f o _ e i _ _	

COMMENTS

This activity can be used to raise awareness of how one sound can have different spellings, for example:

go—know—sew—dough

isle—aisle—file—style—trial

1.15 Explain the word

LEVEL

Intermediate and above

TIME

20–30 minutes

AIMS

To develop familiarity with the *alphabet*; deductive guesswork.

MATERIALS

A dictionary for each group of three or four students.

PROCEDURE

1 Divide the class into small groups and give each group a dictionary. Ask them to open it in the middle. What are the words at the top of the page? Explain what **running heads** are and how they can be useful.

2 Ask the groups to look through the **headwords** on that page for a couple of minutes.

3 One member of each group takes the dictionary and explains one of the headwords by suggesting a context where it could be used but without saying the actual word. Alternatively, he or she could read out the example, but without the key word. The rest of the group must try to remember and call out the word. Once the word has been guessed, the dictionary is passed to another member of the group, who explains another word from the same page. Continue until everyone has had a go.

4 The next stage is more difficult: one group member opens the dictionary at a page of his or her choosing and tells the rest of the group the two running heads. The team brainstorms for a minute to see how many headwords they can think of that fall between the running heads.

5 The person with the dictionary explains one of the headwords that he or she believes the group should know. The examples given to contextualize the headword can also be read out, but with the key word left out. The others try to guess the word. Again, with each correct guess, the dictionary passes to another member of the group.

Example
Reader: The running heads are *episode* and *erode*.
Group: headwords between those words should include: *equal, equality, equipment, equip, equator . . .*
Reader: OK, what's this headword? It means to build something or to put it in a vertical position.
Group: ?
Reader: OK. Here's the example: *Huge television screens were _____ so that everybody could see what was going on.*
Group: *erected?*
Reader: Yes. (Passes the dictionary to the next person.)

(from *Oxford Wordpower Dictionary*, p. 213)

VARIATION

Lower-level students can read out the definitions and the examples.

COMMENTS

Most dictionaries have 'running heads' at the top of the page (i.e. the first and last words on that page), which can help you save time when looking for a word. In dictionaries that do not use running heads, train students to check the first and last complete headwords on the page.

1.16 First and last words

LEVEL

Intermediate and above

TIME

10–20 minutes

AIMS

To familiarize students with the *alphabet*; to help students think about the vocabulary they know.

MATERIALS

A class set of dictionaries.

PROCEDURE

1 Divide the class into five groups. On the board write

A B C D E

F G H I J

K L M N O

P Q R S T

U V W X Y Z

Give each group one set of letters.

2 Explain that each group must guess which is the first and last 'real' word given in the dictionary for each of the letters on their list ('a' and 'b' and abbreviations like BA do not count). They have five minutes to do this without looking at the dictionary.

3 They check their guesses in the dictionary. Were there any surprises?

4 How many of the first and last words were new to the students? Ask them to look at their dictionaries again to find the first and last words they think everyone in the class knows.

FOLLOW-UP

Ask the students to write a short story including at least three first or last words from letters from anywhere in the dictionary. When they have finished, put up the compositions on the walls around the room. Students read each others' work to try to spot the first and last words.

1.17 Anagrams

LEVEL

Intermediate and above

TIME

15–20 minutes

AIMS

To provide spelling practice; to encourage discussion.

MATERIALS

A dictionary for each group of three students. The dictionaries must be the same.

PROCEDURE

1 Write your name up on the board as an anagram. Ask the class whose name it is. When they have done that, explain that they have just worked with an 'anagram'.

2 Divide the class into groups of three. Ask them to choose an interesting page and study it for a few minutes, checking any new words.

3 Each group rewrites the headwords as anagrams on a piece of paper. They must only rewrite the words they could use themselves, and the anagrams should be in the same order as the headwords. The anagrams should also be numbered. On the other side of the piece of paper each group writes clues about the meaning of the chosen anagrams (for example: *something you sit on* or *this is a verb of motion*), and numbers them to match the anagrams.

4 The groups swap pieces of paper and work out the original headwords. If they are having trouble, looking at the clues can help.

5 They check in their dictionary to see if they were right, and to find which words the original group left out, if any.

6 Finally, return the pieces of paper to the original groups. Can they remember their own anagrams?

FOLLOW-UP

Make new groups with one person from each of the original groups, and ask them to write a story using as many of the anagrams as possible. They write the words as anagrams in the story. The groups swap stories and unscramble the anagrams.

VARIATION

You can also use this activity to revise recent vocabulary.

Answers

1.1 A 1 i; 2 g; 3 b; 4 e; 5 c; 6 h; 7 f; 8 j; 9 k; 10 l; 11 d; 12 a
   B 1 c; 2 a; 3 j, l; 4 h, e, b; 5 d; 6 i; 7 g

1.5 1 What does that word mean?
   2 How do you spell it?
   3 How do you pronounce it?
   4 What is the difference between X and Y?
   5 Why don't you look it up in a dictionary?

1.8 B a e i o u
   C 1 y; 2 j; 3 r; 4 d and f; 5 v and w; 6 j; 7 v
   D a b c d e f g h i j k l m n o p q r s t u v w x y z
   E 1 Friday Monday Saturday Sunday Thursday Tuesday Wednesday
      2 April August December February January July June March May November October September

1.9 A 1 b; 2 a; 3 b; 4 b; 5 a; 6 a; 7 a; 8 c; 9 a; 10 a

2 Working with headwords

The activities in this chapter focus on working with **headwords** in various ways, starting with basic word recognition skills (for example, 2.1, 'Hide a page'). An important element of this involves understanding how words are formed, both in terms of **syllables** (for example, 2.2, 'Searching for syllables', page 38) and **affixes** (2.6, 'Fix an affix', page 47).

Part of knowing a word must include knowing how to pronounce it. Several of the activities in this chapter practise pronunciation (for example, 2.8, 'Mouthing words', page 50) and work with **phonemic transcription** (2.10, 'Problem sounds and symbols', page 51) so that students will learn how to pronounce any word they find in a dictionary. Other activities relate sense to sound (2.14, 'Sight and sound,' page 56; 2.15, 'Sounds right', page 57) in **onomatopoeia** and **alliteration**.

The final activities look at the various **codes** and symbols used in dictionary **entries** (2.16, 'Signs and symbols', page 60), including verb codes, which are often a source of mystery to both students and teachers (2.18, 'Verb codes', page 65).

2.1 Hide a page

LEVEL	**Elementary and above**
TIME	**25–35 minutes**
AIMS	**To practise word recognition skills and spelling.**
MATERIALS	An empty wordsearch grid for each pair; a dictionary for each pair.
PREPARATION	Draw a blank grid with 100 squares (10 x 10) and make a copy for every two students (or they can draw it themselves, or use squared paper).
PROCEDURE	1 Put a sample wordsearch on the board or overhead projector (see page 37). Explain that this wordsearch contains a number of hidden words which begin with the same letter and come from the same page of the dictionary. Words could be written horizontally, vertically, or diagonally, and forwards or

backwards. Tell the class the first word on the page. How many words can they find in two minutes?

2 Put the students in pairs and give each pair a blank wordsearch grid, or ask them to draw one.

3 Ask each pair to find a page of their dictionary with at least 15 different headwords. They should all choose a different page and keep it a secret. It doesn't matter if they use different dictionaries.

4 The pairs look through the headwords together, checking how many they know, for a couple of minutes.

5 Ask them to choose at least ten headwords from their page and to write them in their blank grid horizontally, vertically, or diagonally, forwards or backwards, as in the example.

6 They fill the rest of the grid with random letters to 'hide' these headwords in the wordsearch. They write the first and last words on the dictionary page above the wordsearch for guidance. Alternatively, they can write the **running heads** which are printed at the top of the page. (Note that running heads may only give the first and last words for two facing pages, as is the case in the examples below.)

7 Pairs swap completed wordsearches (and dictionaries, if they have used different ones). They have five minutes to find as many of the ten hidden words as possible (lower-level students may need more time).

8 Before the wordsearches are returned, ask everyone to see how many of their own words they can still remember. This concentrates the mind, and when the wordsearches are returned, the original pairs can use them as a memory check.

Examples

The Advanced example is based on the *Oxford Advanced Learner's Dictionary*, 5th edition, p. 674. Running heads: *legged* to *lesson* (p. 675).

The Elementary example is based on the *Longman New Junior English Dictionary*, p. 69. Running heads: *coincidence* (p. 68) to *Commonwealth*.

For the answers, see the end of the chapter, page 67.

Advanced

s	g	n	i	g	g	e	l	j	o
x	v	t	a	g	o	p	e	a	w
a	b	o	d	q	l	e	g	i	t
v	i	n	b	n	v	k	g	f	a
c	e	g	j	o	e	f	y	e	l
l	s	l	e	m	u	r	u	g	h
y	a	t	l	e	g	w	o	r	k
d	o	g	e	l	l	n	f	u	m
l	e	i	s	u	r	e	b	o	g
s	s	e	l	g	e	l	x	b	a

Elementary

c	c	c	o	m	e	d	y	n	o
o	b	c	e	t	y	n	n	u	l
m	a	q	d	r	f	a	v	e	t
m	a	e	t	c	o	m	i	c	n
e	m	o	c	c	a	m	n	o	e
r	x	c	e	b	o	o	y	m	m
c	o	m	m	o	n	c	b	m	m
e	r	o	e	s	d	s	r	a	o
b	e	e	t	t	i	m	m	o	c
c	o	m	f	o	r	t	b	i	c

Photocopiable © Oxford University Press

VARIATION 1

Students can do this task with recently learnt vocabulary, and hide the items for other pairs to find.

VARIATION 2

Ask students to choose a certain topic, as suggested above, and a letter of the alphabet. Instead of hiding ten words from one page, they must look through the entries in the dictionary for that letter until they have found ten associated with the topic, which they should hide in the wordsearch.

2.2 Searching for syllables

LEVEL

False beginners and above

TIME

20–30 minutes

AIMS

To provide practice with *word formation*; to encourage creative thinking; to improve memory.

MATERIALS

A class set of the same dictionary; thin cardboard (optional).

PREPARATION

Select a page in the dictionary where your students should know most of the words, divide the headwords into syllables, and write out all the syllables on a piece of paper. Make a copy for each group of four students (if possible on to thin card), then cut them up so that each syllable is on a different piece of card. Put the cards into sets and shuffle the sets so that they are out of order. An advanced level example is on the next page. The words are taken from the *Oxford Advanced Learner's Dictionary*, p. 383.

PROCEDURE

1 Put the class into groups of four and give each group a set of cards. The students must try to recombine the syllables to make as many words as possible in five minutes. If they are in doubt about whether words exist, they can check in a dictionary. Ask them to list their words in alphabetical order.

2 Put each group together with another group, and ask them to compare their words and discuss the meanings of any new words.

3 Ask the students if they can guess which page of the dictionary you used.

4 Prompt them by writing the first and last headword of the page on the board, and tell them how many other headwords there are. (In the example above the first and last words are *Englishman* and *enormous*, and there are 20 headwords.)

Eng	lish	man	en	grave
en	gulf	en	gross	en
hance	en	ig	ma	en
join	en	joy	en	joy
ment	en	large	en	light
en	en	list	en	liv
en	en	masse	en	mesh
en	mi	ty	en	nob
le	en	nui	en	or
mi	ty	en	orm	ous

5 In their original groups, the students combine the syllables to find as many missing headwords as possible from that page. Set a time limit, which need not be too generous. To check, the groups refer to their dictionaries and again check the meaning of any unknown words.

FOLLOW-UP

Next lesson, distribute the same slips of paper with the same syllables, and ask the class to remember the words. The difference is likely to be impressive.

2.3 Find the noun

LEVEL

Elementary and above

TIME

20 minutes +

AIMS

To practise word building and vocabulary development.

MATERIALS

A copy of the 'Find the noun' worksheet for each student; a dictionary for each pair.

PREPARATION

Copy the worksheet, or make a similar one at your students' level.

PROCEDURE

1 Give out the worksheet and ask the students to complete it without a dictionary. They check their answers in pairs.
2 They then check their answers in the dictionary.

FIND THE NOUN

Elementary

What are the noun forms for these adjectives?

	Adjective	Noun		Adjective	Noun
1	wide	_____	11	daily	_____
2	lazy	_____	12	warm	_____
3	helpful	_____	13	generous	_____
4	sad	_____	14	long	_____
5	gentle	_____	15	hot	_____
6	difficult	_____	16	happy	_____
7	easy	_____	17	real	_____
8	national	_____	18	comfortable	_____
9	expensive	_____	19	practical	_____
10	political	_____	20	soft	_____

FIND THE NOUN

Advanced

What are the noun forms for these adjectives?

Adjective	Noun	Adjective	Noun
1 famous	_____	**11** matrimonial	_____
2 luxurious	_____	**12** essential	_____
3 spacious	_____	**13** proficient	_____
4 ferocious	_____	**14** patient	_____
5 successive	_____	**15** obedient	_____
6 abusive	_____	**16** lenient	_____
7 persuasive	_____	**17** wise	_____
8 compulsive	_____	**18** rare	_____
9 residential	_____	**19** stupid	_____
10 substantial	_____	**20** majestic	_____

Photocopiable © Oxford University Press

(For answers see the 'Find the adjective' worksheets on the next page.)

3 Give each pair of students four or five adjectives to work on. They write three to five short texts using the adjectives and nouns above together (for example, mini-dialogues, sentences, questions and answers, or stories).

   Examples
   It was a very hot day. The heat made everyone feel tired.

   Which is the most comfortable room? I don't know. Comfort isn't important to me.

4 When the students have finished, form new groups so that they can look at examples of all the sentences. Encourage discussion of the different examples.

VARIATION

For more student interaction, you can give half the class the 'Find the adjective' worksheet, and then at the correction stage put pairs with this worksheet together with pairs who have 'Find the noun' worksheets.

FIND THE ADJECTIVE

Elementary

What are the adjective forms of these nouns?

1	width	_____	**11** day	_____
2	laziness	_____	**12** warmth	_____
3	help	_____	**13** generosity	_____
4	sadness	_____	**14** length	_____
5	gentleness	_____	**15** heat	_____
6	difficulty	_____	**16** happiness	_____
7	easiness		**17** reality	_____
	or ease	_____	**18** comfort	_____
8	nation *or*		**19** practice *or*	
	nationality	_____	practicality	_____
9	expense	_____	**20** softness	_____
10	politics	_____		

Photocopiable © Oxford University Press

FIND THE ADJECTIVE

Advanced

What are the adjective forms for these nouns?

1	fame	_____	**11** matrimony	_____
2	luxury	_____	**12** essence	_____
3	space	_____	**13** proficiency	_____
4	ferocity	_____	**14** patience	_____
5	succession	_____	**15** obedience	_____
6	abuse	_____	**16** leniency	_____
7	persuasion	_____	**17** wisdom	_____
8	compulsion	_____	**18** rarity	_____
9	residence	_____	**19** stupidity	_____
10	substance	_____	**20** majesty	_____

Photocopiable © Oxford University Press

2.4 Word sets

LEVEL	**Elementary and above**
TIME	**20 minutes +**
AIMS	**To practise *word formation* and vocabulary development.**
MATERIALS	List of words (see the example on the next page); pieces of card.
PREPARATION	Decide which word sets to use. Copy the list of words overleaf or make a similar one at your students' level. Make enough copies for each player to have two sets of four words. Cut out the words and write or stick each one on to a separate card. If you use card, or can laminate it, the game can be re-used, and that will reduce the cutting and sticking in the future.

PROCEDURE

1 Put the students into groups of 5–6. Explain that they are going to play a game and that each person will receive eight cards, each with a word on. The players have to collect two complete word sets. Each word set has a noun, a verb, an adjective, and an adverb (some with negative forms). Shuffle and deal out the cards, face down, so that each player gets eight.

2 Tell the players to look through their cards and decide which word families to collect. Before the collecting starts, ask each person to predict what the missing members of the word families should be. They can use dictionaries to check their guesses and they should write down their ideas.

3 Now the game starts: each player must choose one word and pass it, face down, to the left. If a player receives a card he or she wants to keep, he or she must pass on a different one from his or her hand.

4 When someone has two complete word sets, they shout 'Stop!' and the game is at an end. (The quick version of the game is to stop with one complete set.)

5 How close were the others to finishing? Can they predict which cards they needed to complete their hands? How many of their guesses in step 2 were correct?

6 Give the groups 5–10 minutes to try to put as many of their words into the context of a story as possible, using a dictionary for guidance. (This can also be done for homework.)

VARIATION

Instead of each person choosing one card to pass on to their neighbour, each player in turn asks another player for a specific card to complete a set: for example, 'Have you got *width*?' If they have, they must hand it over. If not, it's the next player's turn.

Example (Lower-intermediate level)

wide	width	widen	widely
entertaining	entertainment	entertain	entertainingly
nominal	name	nominate	nominally
basic	base	base	basically
decisive	decision	decide	indecisively
productive	product	produce	productively
receptive	reception	receive	receptively
comparative	comparison	compare	comparatively
friendly	friendship	befriend	in a friendly way
argumentative	argument	argue	arguably

repetitive	repetition	repeat	repeatedly
various	variety	vary	invariably
agreeable	agreement	agree	disagreeably
believable	belief	believe	unbelievably
criminal	crime	incriminate	criminally
enthusiastic	enthusiasm	enthuse	enthusiastically
different	difference	differ	differently
satisfied	satisfaction	satisfy	satisfactorily
apparent	appearance	appear	apparently
bored	boredom	bore	boringly

reliable	reliability	rely	unreliably
high	height	heighten	highly
impressive	impression	impress	impressively
soft	softness	soften	softly

2.5 Affixes

LEVEL

Intermediate and above

TIME

15–20 minutes

AIMS

Raising students' awareness of *word formation*; facilitating vocabulary development.

MATERIALS

One dictionary per pair.

PROCEDURE

1 Write the word *happy* on the board. Ask the class how many words they know that have the same **stem**, for example: *happily, unhappy, unhappily, happiness*. Tell the students that they can double their word power by knowing how to use **affixes** (beginnings and endings) such as *un-*, *-ly*, *-y* etc.

2 Put the class into pairs and ask them to think of endings which make nouns from other words. Give them two minutes to think of as many of these endings as they can.

3 They call out the endings they have thought of. Write them up on the board or overhead projector. Ask for examples of words with these endings. Which **suffixes** refer to people? (*-er, -ee, -or, -ian, -ist*) Which refer to abstract qualities? (*-tion, -sion, -ment, -ity, -ness, -y*)

4 The pairs look through dictionaries to find at least two words with each ending. They also see if they can find any endings which are not on the board.

Take feedback again.

FOLLOW-UP

Ask the students to write down the list of endings and to write sentences using a word with each ending. This could be done for homework.

VARIATION

This activity can also be done with other affixes: for example, **prefixes** such as *un-*, *in-*, *pre-*, *ex-*, or suffixes which form verbs from other words, such as *-ify*, *-tate*.

2.6 Fix an affix

LEVEL

Lower-intermediate and above

TIME

20–30 minutes

AIMS

To raise awareness about *affixes* and how they are presented in dictionaries.

MATERIALS

Copies of the worksheet, a dictionary for each pair.

PREPARATION

Make a copy of the 'Beginnings and endings' worksheet for everyone or make a similar one at a suitable level for your class.

PROCEDURE

1 Write the following words on the board or an overhead transparency as a 'word rose', with a question mark in the middle (this will help memory and be a handy way for students to organize their word building).

hope-

thank-   thought-

?

meaning-   grate-

care-

Ask the class to use a dictionary to find what the missing ending is (answer: *-ful*). When they have found it, rub out the question mark and put *-ful* in the centre of the rose. Were the words given their own entries or did they appear as part of another entry? Did the words appear in full or was only the affix given?

2 Give out the worksheet, and ask the students to complete it in pairs.

BEGINNINGS AND ENDINGS

Lower-intermediate

Use your dictionary to see which beginning (prefix) or ending (suffix) the following lists of words have in common.

Example
king   wise   free = king**dom**   wis**dom**   free**dom**

1	risk	wind	health	
2	week	month	day	
3	dark	thick	sweet	deaf
4	legal	logical	literate	
5	improve	entertain	manage	
6	murder	teach	employ	
7	piano	guitar	art	psychology
8	employed	expected	beatable	

Photocopiable © Oxford University Press

3 Check the answers with the class (see the end of the chapter, page 68, for a key). Then ask the pairs to add two more words to each list, either by using the dictionary or from memory.

4 One person from each pair writes the new words on the board—just the **stems**, without any indication of which category they belong to.

5 Erase any duplications. The pairs work quickly to find the right affix for each stem, then check their answers in the dictionary.

2.7   Spot that prefix

LEVEL	**Intermediate and above**
TIME	**20 minutes**
AIMS	**To raise awareness of *prefix* meanings.**
MATERIALS	Copies of the worksheet; a dictionary for each pair.
PREPARATION	Make a copy of the 'Spot that prefix' worksheet for each student, or make your own version at a suitable level for your class.
PROCEDURE	1 Put the students in pairs, and write up the following prefix forms on the board or overhead transparency:

de-   dis-   ill-   in-   pre-

2 Ask the pairs to think what they are and what they mean. Can
   they think of any examples of words that begin with those
   prefixes?
3 Distribute the worksheet, and give the pairs five minutes to
   work through it.

SPOT THAT PREFIX

Intermediate

Look at the lists of words below. In each list there are two words
that are different from the others because they do not start with a
prefix.

a What do the prefixes mean?
b Which are the words that do not belong in the lists?

---

1 deal decline degenerate deliberate detach
2 dishonest disadvantage discipline discourage distance
3 illegal illness illegible illustrate illogical
4 inappropriate inarticulate indeed independent injury
5 preview precocious precious predict pressure

Photocopiable © Oxford University Press

4 Take feedback and ask the students to justify their answers.
   Check that they know the meaning and pronunciation of the
   words (see the end of the chapter, page 68, for an answer key).
5 Ask the pairs to use their dictionaries to add two more words to
   each of the prefix lists and to make a sentence for each genuine
   prefix in order to show the meaning in context.

FOLLOW-UP 1

Get the class to brainstorm more prefixes (or **suffixes**), and write
them up on the board. Ask the pairs to use their dictionaries to
produce a similar list to the one above. They can then either
exchange lists, or put them up on a board for the class to look
through later.

FOLLOW-UP 2

Ask each pair to focus on one line of words from the worksheet.
For each word they find two nouns or adjectives that can combine
with it. Form new groups so that each group has someone who
has worked with each line. The groups discuss their
combinations.

2.8 Mouthing words

LEVEL	**All**
TIME	**10–20 minutes**
AIMS	**To improve pronunciation and word recognition skills.**
MATERIALS	A class set of dictionaries.
PREPARATION	Select a page of the dictionary where the students know most of the words and where there is quite a variety of **headwords**, not simply a list of **derivatives**.
PROCEDURE	1 Put the students into threes, and ask everyone to open the dictionary at the same page. Ask how many new headwords there are, and if the students are unsure of any of the pronunciations. Get the students to look at the **phonemic transcriptions** of the headwords and to guess the pronunciation of any new words.
	2 Either read out the headwords yourself with the class listening, or go round the class with each student reading out one. Correct any problems with pronunciation and meaning.
	3 Explain that you are going to read out one headword again and that the students should write down which word you say. But this time you say it silently—this encourages close attention to your mouth and lip movements. Ask the class which word they 'heard'. Give as many silent repeats as necessary, perhaps building up to a whisper if no answers are forthcoming.
	4 Repeat the process with two or three more words. The groups must agree on what the words were. Take feedback from the class: how many were right?
	5 The students do the same in their groups. They take it in turns to mouth a word for the others to guess.
COMMENTS	This mouthing technique is a good way of helping students correct mistakes with their pronunciation since it helps them focus on their 'inner ear'. It also relates mouth movement to sound very visually.

2.9 Predictable pronunciation

LEVEL	**All**
TIME	**5–10 minutes**
AIMS	**To encourage guesses about pronunciation; to familiarize students with *phonemic symbols*.**

MATERIALS

A class set of dictionaries.

PREPARATION

Choose 5–10 problematic words whose pronunciation you want the class to focus on, perhaps taken from an activity or text they will be studying.

PROCEDURE

1 Write your chosen words on the board or overhead transparency and ask the students, in pairs, to predict how to pronounce them in English.

2 Invite the students to practise with other possibilities: different **stress** patterns, shorter or longer vowel sounds, with lips more rounded, or more relaxed, and so on. However, don't give feedback about the accuracy of their pronunciation. Finally ask which version sounds 'most English' to them.

3 The students check in their dictionaries and compare the versions that sounded most English to them with the **phonemic transcriptions**. Encourage the pairs to practise saying the words correctly together.

VARIATION

Choose a list of words that all have a particular sound—perhaps one the class have had problems with—and mouth them all, one at a time. First ask the class to guess which sound they have in common, then to find the individual words.

Example sounds

/i:/ sheet – meet – street – heat – beat

/ŋ/ singing – bring – hang – honk

COMMENTS

If the students are familiar with the conventions used in the dictionary for stress and transcription, they will quickly learn to assimilate the pronunciation of new words. If they are unfamiliar with phonemic transcriptions, this activity, used little and often, can teach them very quickly.

2.10 Problem sounds and symbols

LEVEL

All

TIME

15 minutes, then ongoing

AIMS

To encourage familiarity with *phonemic symbols*; to provide pronunciation practice.

MATERIALS

A class set of dictionaries.

PREPARATION	Make a list of 5–10 words containing a sound that the class find difficult.

Examples of problem sounds

/w/ as in *woman, which, away, forward, war*

/tʃ/ as in *watch, charge, approach, cheque*

PROCEDURE

1 Write the list of words on the board and ask the students to look them up in their dictionaries and work out the correct pronunciation.

2 Put the students in pairs. Which phonemic symbol occurs in all the words? How is it pronounced? Take feedback and make sure everyone can now pronounce the words correctly.

3 The pairs think of three more words containing the problem sound and write them out with the phonemic symbol replacing the letters that represent the difficulty. Then they check in the dictionary.

FOLLOW-UP

The class keeps a record through the week of all the new words with the problem sound on a display board. It is more memorable if the phonemic symbol is coloured.

2.11 Homophone crosswords

LEVEL

Upper-intermediate and above

TIME

20–30 minutes

AIMS

To practise working with *homophones*; to check spelling; to practise with *phonemic symbols*.

MATERIALS

Two copies of the crossword grid and dictionary for each pair.

PREPARATION

Copy the crosswords below, or make similar ones at your students' level.

PROCEDURE

1 Put the words *here* and *hear* on the board and ask a student to pronounce them. Explain that a homophone is a word pronounced like another word, but with a different meaning or spelling.

2 Put the students in pairs and give each pair two copies of the homophone crosswords so that some have A, some B, and some C in equal numbers.

3 Explain that each of the words in phonemic script has two different spellings. The pairs must find the two homophones in the dictionary and then write clues for each of the two words, one for the team on their right and a different one for the team on their left. The words go across from left to right and down.

4 When they have completed the clues, the pairs pass their homophone crosswords to their neighbours. Using the clues and the phonemic transcriptions, the pairs find the words in their dictionaries and confirm their answers (and the spellings). There is an answer key at the end of the chapter (page 68).

A

[1] f	[2] l	aʊ	ə		
	əʊ				[3] l
	[4] n	ɒ	[5] t		e
			aɪ		n
			[6] m	iː	t

B

[1] p			[2] b	l	uː
[3] eɪ	d		i		
n		[5] ə	l	[6] aʊ	d
			d		eɪ
					z

C

			[1] r	[2] ɔː
[3] p	l	eɪ	n	l
iː				t
s				ə
[4] s	[5] w	iː	t	
	ɔː			

2.12 Phonemic bingo

LEVEL

Elementary and above

TIME

20 minutes +

AIMS

To develop awareness of *phonemic symbols* and practise using them.

MATERIALS

Word list and bingo chart (see step 2); dictionaries.

PREPARATION

Make a list of 20–30 words you would like to present or practise with your class, making sure they do not all sound similar.

PROCEDURE

1 Ask the students to look at the phonemic symbols in their dictionary and to find a long vowel, a short vowel, and a diphthong. Make sure that everyone knows which is which.

2 Divide the class into pairs and ask each pair to draw a 3 x 3 grid. Then they choose a different phonemic symbol to put in each of the nine squares. They must choose two long vowels, two diphthongs, and two short vowels, and then fill the remaining squares with any other symbols. They should leave plenty of space to write words.

Example

æ	əʊ	ɪ
ɔː	ʌ	iː
ʧ	aɪ	θ

Photocopiable © Oxford University Press

3 Explain that you are going to read out some words (or write them on the board). The students have to listen out for their sounds and try to complete their grid. Every time they hear a word with one of their sounds in, they write it in that square. Each word can only be used once, so that, for example, /kæt/ represents either /k/, /æ/, or /t/.

4 Dictate your words slowly; the students fill in their squares as you go. The winners are the first pair to complete the grid.

COMMENTS

You can use this activity to practise sounds the students have problems producing or differentiating.

2.13 Stress patterns

LEVEL	Intermediate and above
TIME	30–40 minutes
AIMS	To help students recognize *stress* markers.
MATERIALS	A copy of the 'Stress sentences' worksheet for each student; a dictionary for each pair.
PROCEDURE	1 Write up the word *object* on the board. In pairs, the students think of as many sentences as possible using the word. Take feedback. Did they use all of its meanings?

2 Listen for what they say: *'object* or *ob'ject*? Say both versions and ask the students to listen to the difference. Can they hear it? What is the difference in meaning? How would the difference be shown in a dictionary?

3 Write the two different stress patterns on the board like this:

●   ·   ·   ●

and explain what they represent. The students check in the dictionary to see which pattern is appropriate for the examples they gave in step 1.

4 Ask the pairs to work through the handout together, checking the meanings of the different stress patterns in the dictionary.

STRESS SENTENCES

The following words all have two stress patterns. What are they?

Can you find the rule that governs this stress pattern?

A record	protest	exploit	discount
B permit	survey	transport	present
C rebel	desert	insult	export
D increase	produce	contract	refund

Photocopiable © Oxford University Press

5 Put pairs together into fours to compare their answers. (The answer is that the stress pattern is ● · for the noun form and · ● for the verb form.)

6 Ask the pairs to write a short text—or a collection of sentences—using both the noun and verb forms together, for example:

That record wasn't worth recording. It's rubbish.

2.14 Sight and sound

LEVEL	**Upper-intermediate and above**
TIME	**20 minutes +**
AIMS	**To raise awareness of *onomatopoeic* effects and sight or sound word groups.**
MATERIALS	A copy of the 'Sight and sound' worksheet for each student; a dictionary for each group of three.
PROCEDURE	

1 Dramatically drop a book, or slam the door. Ask what the students heard and how they would describe the sound—elicit words like *bang*, *crash*. Explain that often English—like all languages—makes use of the sound of groups of letters to suggest things we see or hear.

2 Write on the board or overhead projector:

   pop, splash, buzz, crunch, tick-tock, crack, thud, moo, ding-dong, cock-a-doodle-do.

   Divide the class into groups of three and ask them to work out what the sounds represent. Explain that there are at least two animal sounds included.

3 Go over the various answers, asking for justifications. Can anyone guess what animals are? (Bee—*buzz*; cow—*moo*; cockerel—*cock-a-doodle-doo*). If you have a multinational group, go round the class comparing animal noises for a moment—there are often amusing differences. If there are doubts or disagreements about the sounds, ask the groups to check in a dictionary to see who is right.

   Ask which sound is like:
   eating an apple? (*crunch*)
   a clock? (*tick-tock*)
   a doorbell? (*ding-dong* or *buzz*)
   breaking a nut? (*crack*)
   opening champagne? (*pop*)
   falling in water? (*splash*)
   a heavy object falling? (*thud*)

4 Give out the copies of the worksheet and ask the groups to work through it without dictionaries.

5 They check their answers in a dictionary: how many did they guess correctly? (See the answer key at the end of the chapter, page 68.) What helped them come to their conclusions?

SIGHT AND SOUND

1 Divide the following words into two lists depending on whether they refer to something you see or something you hear:

shine	clank	sparkle	tinkle	gleam
glitter	clatter	crash	shimmer	whizz
swish	glisten	clunk	glow	jangle
blare	twinkle	boom	crackle	

Sight	**Sound**	**Cause or context?**

2 Think of one context for each verb and write it in the cause column above.

3 Which combinations of letters create an impression of noise? Why?

Photocopiable © Oxford University Press

FOLLOW-UP

Students work in pairs and write the diary of either (a) a person with a splitting headache, or (b) someone on the beach, ... using as many of the words as possible. This could be done individually for homework.

2.15 Sounds right

LEVEL

Upper-intermediate and above

TIME

30–40 minutes with both worksheets

AIMS

To help students to appreciate the 'sound' of English; vocabulary development and awareness of register.

MATERIALS

A copy of the 'Sounds right' worksheets for each student; a dictionary for each pair.

PROCEDURE

1 Explain that there are many expressions in English which depend on sound similarities of one sort or another, such as **alliteration**: *time and tide, there and then, good as gold, cool as a cucumber*; and rhyme: *by hook or by crook, make or break*.

2 Put the students in pairs and give each person a copy of worksheet 1. Ask them to guess what the rhyming words could be, then check in a dictionary. (There is an answer key at the end of the chapter, page 68.)

3 Take feedback. Did they manage to find all the words? How many of their guesses were correct? What did they notice about the register of the expressions? Which ones are informal, and why? (Normally rhyme is used for emphasis and is often combined with a forceful position—often negative or humorous—which is why most of these expressions are quite dismissive. *Hustle and bustle* and, to a lesser degree, *hurly-burly* are used for more poetic effect.)

4 Give out worksheet 2, and check that everyone understands how alliterative expressions work: the first consonant(s) is repeated in the second element or word, and the consonants at the end of the word tend to be repeated, too. But be careful—these are not rhymes. Then it's a matter of guessing which new vowel sound replaces the original sound. Ask the pairs to try and predict what the second word is likely to be.

5 After a few minutes of guessing, let the pairs check in a dictionary. How many of their answers were good guesses? Check that everyone understands the meaning and register of the expressions. Now quickly drill the correct pronunciation of the expressions around the class (this is important).

6 The pairs write out sentences which provide contexts for their favourite two or three alliterative expressions, leaving a blank where the expression should go. Then they read their sentences to the class, and everyone shouts out the appropriate alliterative expressions in chorus.

COMMENTS

Shouting out alliterative expressions in chorus is fun, and also important practice of something that absolutely depends on perfect pronunciation to be comprehensible. This technique provides a lot of practice of the same items with variety—each pair will produce a different context. It also makes students listen to one another. You may also want to do some individual drilling and checking as individual students cannot be heard in a chorus.

SOUNDS RIGHT   1

Complete the following expressions by guessing what the rhyming sound should be.

1 He's a **fuddy-**_____ .

2 He said some **mumbo-**_____ about the type of legal contract we had to sign.

3 We only got down to the real **nitty-**_____ after an hour of making polite conversation.

4 How can you find anything in here with your books and files all **higgledy-**_____?

5 You can't just make everyone do the same work **willy-**_____

6 He's not the fattest person I know, but he is a little **roly-**_____

7 Not everyone enjoys the **hurly-**_____ of noisy parties.

8 On Friday evening there's nothing I look forward to more than the chance to escape the **hustle and** _____ of the city.

9 It's true: she does travel a lot on business, but I don't think she gets up to any **hanky-**_____ while she's away.

10 The politician said some **clap**_____ about what his party promised for the future, but I don't think anyone really believed him.

SOUNDS RIGHT   2

Use your dictionary to complete the following alliterative expressions, and then make a sentence using each one. Notice that the first and last sounds are the same, as in *ping-pon*g.

1	flip-_____	6	chit-_____
2	tit for _____	7	zig_____
3	wishy-_____	8	tip_____
4	shilly-_____	9	ding-_____
5	mish_____	10	topsy-_____

2.16 Signs and symbols

LEVEL

Elementary and above

TIME

10 minutes +

AIMS

To raise awareness of the meaning of non-linguistic symbols used in dictionaries.

MATERIALS

A dictionary for each pair.

PROCEDURE

1 Ask the class to brainstorm in pairs what they can find in dictionaries *apart* from words. Encourage the class to think beyond the obvious answer of 'pictures or illustrations'.

2 Discuss the answers. If no-one suggests it, ask about the symbols used—perhaps draw an exclamation mark on the board and ask where they might find that in the dictionary. Other examples are: arrows, dashes, exclamation marks, circles, squares, diamonds, stars, =, ~, ▶, ✶, ☛, ⇨.

3 In pairs, the students look for somewhere where the signs and symbols are explained (probably at the front or back of the dictionary). Ask them to find examples of each symbol. How many can they find, and what sort of information comes before and after them?

4 Put the pairs into fours to compare notes. If they are using different dictionaries, they should compare and contrast what they have found.

5 After a few minutes, ask one person from each group to come up to the board and draw the signs and symbols they have found. Don't worry if some are the same—this will reinforce the message and show the importance of certain signs.

6 Each student makes a list of the symbols and their meanings in his or her dictionary for future reference. This can also be done as a wall display.

2.17 Dictionary codes

LEVEL

Lower-intermediate and above

TIME

60 minutes

AIMS

To familiarize students with the style of dictionary entries; to help them understand the various *codes* and *abbreviations* found in dictionaries.

MATERIALS

A copy of the 'Codes, symbols, and abbreviations' worksheet for each student; a dictionary for each pair.

PREPARATION

Make copies of the worksheets or prepare a similar one suitable for your students.

PROCEDURE

1 Ask the students to brainstorm what they find in dictionaries apart from definitions and meanings. Give them a minute or two. Take feedback. If nobody suggests abbreviations and codes, ask how they know if a word is British English or American English, if it is regular or irregular, a noun or a verb.

2 Once the idea of codes has been established, ask pairs to think of as many examples as possible of codes and abbreviations they might find in the dictionary. After two or three minutes, ask them to compare their ideas in fours. Do they now have more than ten different examples?

3 Divide the class into six groups: A, B, C, D, E, and F, or into groups of four if you have a class with more than 30, and give each student the worksheet for that group. If you are using the lower-intermediate worksheet, divide the groups into five groups: A, B, C, D, and E. How many of the items on their list have they already mentioned?

4 The students discuss what the abbreviations mean, then check in a dictionary. (There is an answer key on page 68.)

5 The groups look for and write down two examples of each item. Circulate to give help, and prompt where necessary. If their dictionaries have different abbreviations for the same codes, they should adapt the worksheet and look for those codes.

6 When the students have completed their worksheets, form new groups with two people from A, B, and C together, and two people from D, E, and F together. With lower-level groups, form new groups with two people from A, B, and C, and also C, D, and E. They compare notes and explain what they have found. Ask them to produce an alphabetical list of their combined abbreviations and codes.

7 Ask a volunteer from an ABC group to come to the board and write the codes along the top of the board in one colour. Then do the same with someone from DEF, but using a different colour.

8 Another volunteer writes up the words they found where the abbreviations were used—but they should not mention what the abbreviations or codes were.

9 Give the groups five minutes to try to match the words on the board with the codes and abbreviations.

10 They check in their dictionaries to see if they were right.

Examples
Advanced level

CODES, SYMBOLS, AND ABBREVIATIONS   A

1 What do you think these codes and abbreviations mean?

abbr	n	arch	pt
conj	sl	joc	techn

2 Can you find a list of abbreviations in your dictionary?

3 Are all these abbreviations included in your list?

4 Find two examples of each of the abbreviations above. Write down the words where you found them.

CODES, SYMBOLS, AND ABBREVIATIONS   B

1 What do you think these codes and abbreviations mean?

adj	U	NZ	aux
esp	pref	neg	illus

2 Can you find a list of abbreviations in your dictionary?

3 Are all these abbreviations included?

4 Find two examples of each of the abbreviations above. Write down the words where you find them.

CODES, SYMBOLS, AND ABBREVIATIONS   C

1 What do you think these codes and abbreviations mean?

US	emph	pl	adv
det	fig	masc	pron

2 Can you find a list of abbreviations in your dictionary?

3 Are all these abbreviations included?

4 Find two examples of each of the abbreviations above. Write down the words where you find them.

CODES, SYMBOLS, AND ABBREVIATIONS   D

1 What do you think these codes and abbreviations means?

fml	pers	suff	C
v	Brit	sb	euph

2 Can you find a list of abbreviations in your dictionary?

3 Are all these abbreviations included?

4 Find two examples of each of the abbreviations above. Write down the words where you find them.

CODES, SYMBOLS, AND ABBREVIATIONS   E

1 What do you think these codes and abbreviations mean?

phr v   possess usu   infml

pp   sth   interrog propr

2 Can you find a list of abbreviations in your dictionary?

3 Are all these abbreviations included?

4 Find two examples of each of the abbreviations above. Write down the words where you find them.

CODES, SYMBOLS, AND ABBREVIATIONS   F

1 What do you think these codes and abbreviations mean?

pres p   U   sing   derog

Scot   prep   idm   reflex

2 Can you find a list of abbreviations in your dictionary?

3 Are all these abbreviations included?

4 Find two examples of each of the abbreviations above. Write down the words where you find them.

(From the *Oxford Advanced Learner's Dictionary*)

Lower-intermediate

CODES, SYMBOLS, AND ABBREVIATIONS   A

1 What do you think these codes and abbreviations mean?

abbr   C   pp   det   eg

2 Can you find a list of abbreviations in your dictionary?

3 Are all these abbreviations included?

4 Find two examples of each of the abbreviations. Write down the words where you find them.

CODES, SYMBOLS, AND ABBREVIATIONS   B

1 What do you think these codes and abbreviations mean?

adj   U   pt   sb   interj

2 Can you find a list of abbreviations in your dictionary?

3 Are all these abbreviations included?

4 Find two examples of each of the abbreviations. Write down the words where you find them.

CODES, SYMBOLS, AND ABBREVIATIONS   C

1 What do you think these codes and abbreviations mean?

adv   pres   US   sth   ie

2 Can you find a list of abbreviations in your dictionary?

3 Are all these abbreviations included?

4 Find two examples of each of the abbreviations. Write down the words where you find them.

CODES, SYMBOLS, AND ABBREVIATIONS   D

1 What do you think these codes and abbreviations mean?

I   comp   etc   prep   conj

2 Can you find a list of abbreviations in your dictionary?

3 Are all these abbreviations included?

4 Find two examples of each of the abbreviations. Write down the words where you find them.

CODES, SYMBOLS, AND ABBREVIATIONS   E

1 What do you think these codes and abbreviations mean?

3rd pers sing   T   pron   pl   pres part

2 Can you find a list of abbreviations in your dictionary?

3 Are all these abbreviations included?

4 Find two examples of each of the abbreviations. Write down the words where you find them.

(From the *Oxford Wordpower Dictionary*)

COMMENTS

1 This is a long activity, but time spent becoming familiar with dictionary codes is always well spent. It does not matter what dictionary the students have, nor if there are variations among the abbreviations, as this is an important insight in itself. Students should be encouraged to work with the abbreviations and codes in the dictionaries that they use most often.

2 See the Glossary (page 164) for explanations of dictionary terms.

2.18 Verb codes

LEVEL	**Elementary to upper-intermediate**
TIME	**25 minutes +**
AIMS	**To raise awareness about the verb *codes* and grammatical information in dictionaries.**
MATERIALS	A dictionary and worksheet for each student.
PREPARATION	Make a copy of the 'Verb codes' worksheet for each student, or a similar worksheet at a suitable level.
PROCEDURE	1 Give out the worksheet, and ask students to work through it in pairs.
	2 Ask the pairs to justify their answers by finding examples in their dictionaries which correspond to the correct grammar patterns.
	3 Take feedback, and discuss any problems. (There is an answer key at the end of the chapter, page 69.)
FOLLOW-UP 1	Divide the class into pairs and give each pair either list a, b, c, d, or e. Ask them to create similar worksheets to the one above.

a say	speak	talk	tell
b buy	spend	sell	cost
c win	save	gain	earn
d like	enjoy	amuse	please
e advise	suggest	offer	recommend

When they are ready, the pairs swap worksheets.

FOLLOW-UP 2	When you correct homework, indicate all errors of verb patterns with the code used in the class dictionary, but do not provide the correction. Make a note of the problem verbs and write them on the board in the next lesson. Ask the class to look up the relevant verb codes. Return the homework and ask the students to make the corrections.

VERB CODES

Look at the entries for these verbs in your dictionary:

say   explain   tell   ask

1 What information is given about the grammatical structures used with the verbs?

Copy the grammatical information for each verb.

2 Look at the examples given for each verb. What do the grammar codes and symbols mean?

3 Using the grammatical information in the dictionary, decide which of these sentences contain mistakes, and correct them.

a Can I ask you a question?
b How much did that cost? Don't ask.
c Please say me the answer.
d Could you explain me the answer again?
e I'm sorry, I haven't got time to explain now.
f What did you tell to her?
g Be quiet, I'm trying to tell a story them.
h Did you tell her that you won't go to the party?
i Please say hello to your mother for me.
j It's difficult to say how old the church is.
k It's difficult to tell how old any church is, in fact.
l If he asks you a question, tell nothing.
m Jane said me she was coming later.
n If you're thirsty, just ask another drink.

2.19 The grammar of words

LEVEL	**Elementary to upper-intermediate**
TIME	**30 minutes +**
AIMS	**To encourage careful reading of dictionary entries for grammatical information.**
MATERIALS	A dictionary for each pair of students—different ones if possible; paper.
PROCEDURE	1 Elicit from the class the sort of words that sometimes cause grammar problems: *although*, *even if*, *despite*, *nevertheless*, *hardly*, *though*, and *whatever* are good at intermediate level and above, while elementary students often have difficulty with *never*, *often*, *well*, *good*, *quite*, *very*, *much*, *many*, *more*, *less*, and *fewer*. Write about ten on the board or overhead projector. Other grammar areas include phrasal verbs, **countable** and **uncountable nouns**, and adverbs.

2 Put the students in pairs and ask them to discuss which words they find the most difficult to use, and what problems they have with them. Then they should look up the problem words in their dictionaries.

3 They copy at least three example sentences from the dictionary on to a piece of paper, but leaving the key 'structure' word as a blank.

4 The pairs swap pieces of paper and try to fill in the gaps. Then they pass the pieces of paper to another pair—not the original writers—for checking. They can correct answers they disagree with.

5 The pieces of paper are passed to the original pairs for final checking. Ask for general feedback about what they have learnt and any problems they had. Did the examples make the use and meaning of the words clear? Can they think of better examples?

Answers

2.1 Advanced wordsearch
Across: leggings, legit, lemur, legwork, lego, leisure, legless
Down: lemon, leggy
Diagonal: lend
Elementary wordsearch
Across: comedy, comic, come, common, committee, comfort
Down: commerce, command, comma, comment

2.6 **1** -y; **2** -ly; **3** -en; **4** il-; **5** -ment; **6** -er; **7** -ist; **8** un-

2.7 deal deliberate; discipline distance; illness illustrate; indeed injury; precious pressure

2.11 A *Across* **1** flower or flour   *Down* **2** lone or loan
                    4 knot or not   **3** leant or lent
                    6 meet or meat   **5** thyme or time

B *Across* **2** blue or blew   *Down* **1** pain or pane
               3 aide or aid   **2** billed or build
               5 aloud or allowed   **6** daze or days

C *Across* **1** raw or roar   *Down* **2** altar or alter
               3 plane or plain   **3** piece or peace
               4 suite or sweet   **5** war or wore

2.14 1 *sight*:   shine, sparkle, gleam, glitter, shimmer, glisten, glow, twinkle

       sound: clank, clatter, crash, whizz, swish, clunk, jangle, blare, boom, crackle, tinkle

       cause/context: many!

3 In English, long vowels, deep vowels, and consonant clusters like /ŋk/ and /kr/ sound loud, while high vowels and /ʃ/ sounds seem quiet.

2.15 1 **1** fuddy-duddy; **2** mumbo-jumbo; **3** nitty-gritty; **4** higgledy-piggledy; **5** willy-nilly; **6** roly-poly; **7** hurly-burly; **8** hustle and bustle; **9** hanky-panky; **10** claptrap

2 **1** flip-flop; **2** tit for tat; **3** wishy-washy; **4** shilly-shally; **5** mishmash; **6** chit-chat; **7** zigzag; **8** tip-top; **9** ding-dong; **10** topsy-turvy

2.17 Advanced

A1 abbreviation, noun, archaic [old-fashioned], past tense, conjunction, slang, jocular [joking], technical

B1 adjective, uncountable noun, New Zealand, auxiliary, especially, prefix, negative, illustration

C1 American usage, emphatic, plural, adverb, determiner, figurative, masculine, pronoun

D1 formal, person, suffix, countable noun, verb, British usage, somebody, euphemistic

E1 phrasal verb, possessive, usually, informal, past participle, something, interrogative, proprietary [brand name]

F1 present participle, uncountable noun, singular, derogatory, Scottish, preposition, idiom, reflexive

Lower-intermediate

A1 abbreviation, countable noun, past participle, determiner, for example

B1 adjective, uncountable noun, past tense, somebody, interjection

C1 adverb, present tense, American English, something, in other words

D1 intransitive, comparative, and so on, preposition, conjunction

E1 third person singular, transitive, pronoun, plural, present participle

2.18 3 c Please tell me the answer.

    d Could you explain the answer to me again?
Or: Could you explain the answer again?

    f What did you tell her?

    g Be quiet, I'm trying to tell them a story.
Or: I'm trying to tell a story.

    l If he asks you a question, say nothing.
Or: tell him nothing.

    m Jane told me she was coming later.
Or: Jane said she was coming later.

    n If you're thirsty, just ask for another drink.

3 Working with meaning

The activities in this chapter are designed to help students interpret and understand what they find once they have got to the right entry in a dictionary.

Students sometimes get no further than repeating a dictionary definition with little idea of what it means, and the examples, instead of enlightening, cause further confusion. Activities like 3.4, 'Quick quiz' (page 75) and 3.6, 'Five true, five false' (page 77) encourage close reading of entries.

Common problems include choosing which meaning of a word is appropriate in a certain context, and working out the sense of the definition given. 3.10, 'More than one meaning' (page 82) and 3.11, 'Multi-meaning bluff' (page 84) look at **homographs** and **homonyms**, while 3.9, 'Words that go together' (page 81) looks at **collocation** and encourages students to learn words in meaningful combinations, rather than in isolation.

One of the keys to successful vocabulary learning is to create connections and **word associations** that make words more memorable and more meaningful. By imposing their own reading on a page, students become more assertive users of the dictionary and learn to assimilate rather than simply repeat the information they come across. 3.15, 'Collapsing a page' (page 88) and 3.16, 'Arguing for words' (page 89) both help students to work in this manner.

3.1 Dictionary ice-breakers

LEVEL	**Elementary and above**
TIME	**10–15 minutes**
AIMS	**To 'warm up' students and encourage discussion; can also be used to form pairs.**
MATERIALS	A dictionary for each pair or student.
PROCEDURE	1 Put the students in pairs and ask them to open the dictionary at random. If you have enough dictionaries, they can work alone with a dictionary each. Ask them to find a word they find particularly interesting on their page, whether new or not.
	2 The students write the word on a piece of paper, then circulate around the class, telling each other their words and listening to

other students to find the person whose word forms the best 'partnership' with theirs. They must listen to everybody before making their decision about the best match. Everyone must find a partner; with an odd number of students, there must be one threesome. This encourages debate and justification.

Possible partnerships:
– *words beginning with the same sound*
– *words we saw yesterday*
– *words connected with sport*
– *negative words*
– *adjectives*
– *words that sound the same in my language*

3 When they have paired up, the students invent three different contexts for their word partnerships. These can then be written up as homework.

3.2 It's a sort of . . .

LEVEL	**Elementary to intermediate**
TIME	**30 minutes**
AIMS	**To provide practice with the structure *It's a sort of …*; to relate new words to known categories (*superordinates*); to help with skimming.**
MATERIALS	A list of words for each and a dictionary for each pair.
PREPARATION	Choose five categories and think of six words from each. Group them into lists of one word from each category, and make enough copies for each pair of students to have one list. In the example on page 72 (for intermediate level), each pair receives one column, either A, B, C, D, E, or F.
PROCEDURE	1 Explain that often students do not need to know the exact meaning of every new word—it's enough to know what the general sense is. Write on the board:

Jim looked out into the garden and watched the tall x, y, and z blowing in the wind. Then he admired the beautiful colours of the a, b, and c that grew all around the garden.

Let the students make guesses about what x, y, and z, and a, b, and c could be for a few seconds, then elicit answers with the question: 'what sort of thing is . . .?'

kind

type

2 Explain that this is a very handy way of paraphrasing or explaining a new word. Put the students into pairs and distribute the lists of words. Ask them to check what sort of

A	B	C	D	E	F
daisy	pansy	daffodil	primrose	carnation	buttercup
trout	owl	salmon	haddock	tuna	crane
bungalow	houseboat	walnut	mansion	willow	semi
beech	cod	bedsit	elm	penthouse	herring
starling	chestnut	crow	sparrow	hawk	oak

things the words on their lists are. Give them five minutes to check in their dictionaries.

3 Ask *What are the five sorts of thing on the list?*

4 Explain that lists A, B, C, D, E, and F have words from the same categories (bird, tree, fish, type of housing, and flower), but are not all in the same order. Ask the pairs to stand up and circulate to find which other pair has the same categories in the same order. They do this by explaining what sort of things their words are, not by translating! (For the answers, see the key at the end of the chapter, page 90.)

FOLLOW-UP

Ask the pairs to produce a similar set of categories for the rest of the class.

3.3 It's got something to do with . . .

LEVEL

Lower-intermediate and above

TIME

20 minutes

AIMS

To teach a key coping structure; to encourage students to relate words to topics.

MATERIALS

Copies of the 'It's got something to do with . . .' worksheet; a dictionary for each pair.

PREPARATION

Make enough copies of the worksheet for each student, or design one at a suitable level for your students.

PROCEDURE

1 Write *chalk*, *blackboard*, *homework*, and *grammar* on the board. Ask the students to say what they have in common. Elicit: *they* **have** all **got something to do with** *teaching, learning, English, or school.*

2 Distribute the worksheet, and ask the students to complete it in pairs. Give them a few minutes to relate the words to the topics by guesswork, using the structure '*I think it's got something to do with . . .*'.

3 Ask them to check their guesses in the dictionary and compare them with another pair.

4 Check the answers (see the answer key at the end of the chapter, page 90).

5 Ask the pairs to think of a specialized topic they are interested in, and vocabulary associated with it. They write a list of four or five words and pass them to their neighbours, who must check in the dictionary to find what the topic is, then add two more words to the list, and continue around the class.

IT'S GOT SOMETHING TO DO WITH ...

Advanced

How fast can you match these words to the topics they are associated with? Use your dictionary to help you.

bole	whisk	sautéed	sub poena	clapper-board
sap	gilts	foliage	cardiology	sound effects
VDU	batter	dividend	hard drive	constituency
ROM	stocks	close-up	the cabinet	a white paper

1			has got something to do with medicine
2	3	4	have got something to do with trees
5	6	7	have got something to do with computers
8	9	10	have got something to do with filming
11	12	13	have got something to do with cooking
14	15	16	have got something to do with British politics
17	18	19	have got something to do with investments
20			has got something to do with the law

Photocopiable © Oxford University Press

IT'S GOT SOMETHING TO DO WITH ...

Lower-intermediate

How fast can you match these words to the topics they are associated with? Use your dictionary to help you.

modem	migraine	whiskers	temperature	monitor
track	gear	kennel	half-time	trailer

1		has got something to do with driving
2	3	have got something to do with animals
4	5	have got something to do with sports
6	7	have got something to do with health
8	9	have got something to do with computers
10		has got something to do with films

Photocopiable © Oxford University Press

3.4 Quick quiz

LEVEL

Elementary and above

TIME

10–15 minutes

AIMS

Vocabulary development; to provide practice with *wh-*questions; to help with contextualizing new vocabulary.

MATERIALS

A quiz worksheet for each student; a set of class dictionaries.

PREPARATION

Prepare a quiz with seven *wh-* questions based on useful items in the dictionary, and copy it for each student.

Example

QUICK QUIZ
Upper-intermediate

1 Where is the *nape* of your neck?
2 What is a *jingle* for?
3 Which illness makes you itch—*chicken pox* or *mumps*?
4 Who wears a *nappy*?
5 When do you find *puddles*?
6 Why do people sign *petitions*?
7 How do you feel when you're *flustered*?

Photocopiable © Oxford University Press

PROCEDURE

1 Give each pair of students a copy of the quiz and ask them how many answers they know already. Don't let them shout out what the answers are!

2 They use their dictionaries to find the answers as quickly as possible: it's a race against the rest of the class.

3 The first pair to finish shout 'Time!' and everyone must close their dictionaries immediately. The pair come to the front of the class.

4 The pair who finished explain the answers, and answer any questions or doubts that the other members of the group may have. The other pairs can challenge them or ask them for another example at any time.

COMMENTS

1 You can use this technique to introduce or preview new vocabulary necessary for reading or listening to a text.

2 A good follow-up is to go on to 3.5, 'Class questions'.

3.5 Class questions

LEVEL

Elementary and above

TIME

5 minutes +

AIMS

To provide practice with *wh-* questions; to help with contextualizing and explaining vocabulary; to 'warm up' the class.

MATERIALS

A piece of paper for each student; a class set of dictionaries.

PROCEDURE

1 Ask each student to look through the dictionary, and to write one question beginning with *Where* about a word they find. You can stipulate another *wh-* word, but everyone should write the same type of question. For example:

   – *Where would you find a ...?*
   – *Where would you use a ...?*
   – *Where does ... grow or come from?*
   – *Where do people say ...?*
   – *Where does a ... work or live?*

With a lower-level group, you might find it profitable to brainstorm these types of questions, or even to ask the class to concentrate on one example, and all to write that type of question.

2 Each student swaps questions with their neighbour, and looks up the answers—but they shouldn't write the answers. The pairs discuss their answers and see if they agree. Once they have reached agreement, they swap their questions with another pair.

3 Continue for five minutes or until you are ready to go on to another part of the lesson. You do not have to let everyone answer every question: if you decide to draw a halt to the activity early, simply take in the slips of paper with the questions and stick them up on the wall or board and tell the class that they must know the answer by the next lesson.

FOLLOW-UP

You can focus on a different type of question at the start of the next lesson.

COMMENTS

This works well as a follow-up to 3.4, 'Quick quiz' (page 75) and is a useful way of starting the class gently, or while waiting for people to arrive at the beginning of a lesson.

3.6 Five true, five false

LEVEL   **Elementary and above**

TIME   **30–40 minutes**

AIMS   **To practise general dictionary skills; to encourage familiarity with the range of information in dictionaries.**

MATERIALS   A worksheet and a dictionary per pair of students.

PREPARATION   Make a copy of the 'Five true, five false' worksheet for everyone, or make a similar one suitable for your students.

PROCEDURE
1 Give the students the worksheet and ask them to complete it in pairs, using a dictionary for guidance.
2 Check the answers (see the key at the end of the chapter, page 90) and ask the students how they found this activity. Was it difficult?
3 Tell the pairs to make a similar worksheet with ten questions using one double-page of the dictionary. They can all work on the same page or—particularly at more advanced levels—on different ones. There must be at least one question about: spelling, meaning, pronunciation, and grammar.
4 Monitor as the pairs produce their worksheets and help with any problems.

FIVE TRUE, FIVE FALSE

Elementary

Five of these statements are TRUE, and five are FALSE. Which is which?

1 *Deer* and *sheep* have no plural form.
2 *Fast–faster–fastest* are comparative and superlative forms, with *fastly* as the adverb.
3 *Disagreed* has four syllables.
4 People can be *middle-aged*.
5 You can meet a friend *in midnight*.
6 *Loft* and *basement* mean the same.
7 An *escalator* will take you to another floor in a building.
8 *Comb* has a silent letter.
9 The correct spelling of the group of politicians who run a country is *governement*.
10 The sky can be *cloudy*.

FIVE TRUE, FIVE FALSE

Intermediate

Five of these statements are TRUE and five are FALSE. Which is which?

1 You can suffer from *exhaust* if you work too hard.

2 *Finger* can be a verb.

3 Clothes can be *auburn*.

4 *Captain* has second syllable stress.

5 *Tough* rhymes with *puff*.

6 You can *break* a bone and a promise.

7 *Cookie* is American.

8 You should *rince* the washing up.

9 *Friendly* is an adjective and an adverb.

10 The noun *progress* has no plural.

FIVE TRUE, FIVE FALSE

Advanced

Five of these statements are TRUE and five are FALSE. Which is which?

1 You can *dabble on* politics.

2 You can't work for twelve hours *continually*.

3 *Freckles* is a disease.

4 *Flashy* is not a compliment.

5 A *windowpane* is a kind of window.

6 You should *face up with* your problems.

7 *Carousel* and *gazelle* rhyme.

8 *Bunny* is a word used by children.

9 If you *stop dead* you die.

10 *Feedback* is an uncountable noun.

Photocopiable © Oxford University Press

5 The pairs swap finished worksheets with their neighbours and answer them. This can be done for homework.

3.7 One new fact

LEVEL
Intermediate and above

TIME
10–15 minutes

AIMS
Vocabulary development.

MATERIALS
A dictionary for each pair.

PREPARATION
Check the dictionary for possible 'new' information about the words you have selected as a focus.

PROCEDURE

1 Divide the class into pairs, and elicit a number of really simple words that they frequently use. Examples could be:

good	*nice*	*get*	*day*	*important*
easy	*white*	*book*	*sky*	*school*
happy	*man*	*animal*	*bad*	*comfortable*
food	*idea*	*understand*	*problem*	*go*
sad	*fat*			

2 Each pair chooses two words from the list and discusses what they know about the words, when and how they use them, when they used them last, and so on. This builds a profile of the words in their minds.

3 After a minute, ask the pairs to look up their words in the dictionary to find one fact that they didn't know before about each one: it could be a **collocation**, an **idiom**, or a grammatical fact—anything at all! They will need a few minutes, because the new facts are often 'buried' in the middle of long entries. Make sure they discuss what they discover and understand it.

4 Ask if every pair has managed to find out something new about their words. If anyone hasn't, make a note of their words on the board. If they all have, ask the pairs to form fours and share what they have discovered, referring to the dictionaries if necessary.

5 The pairs circulate and swap information.

6 Conduct feedback: what were the biggest surprises? Is the new fact easy to understand, or the new meaning or example easy to use?

7 If someone has not managed to discover something new, congratulate them on knowing all the uses of the word!

COMMENTS
This is a useful activity for when students are drifting into class. Students are often amazed at discoveries concerning 'simple' words that they thought they knew all about. It is a good idea to have a few 'facts' up your sleeve beforehand—be sure to check the

dictionary before you start the activity. Examples for the words above could include:

happy-go-lucky *white lie* *that'll do nicely*
call it a day *easy does it* *a school of fish*
to feel important *a baddie* *sky blue*
it's no good telling me now

You can either present these as a worksheet, inviting students to find out what they mean, or you could circulate round the class, 'giving' pairs such expressions where appropriate.

3.8 Question grid

LEVEL   **Elementary and above**

TIME   **30 minutes**

AIMS   **To provide skills practice; to revise question formation; vocabulary development.**

MATERIALS   A dictionary for each group of 3–4 students.

PROCEDURE   1 Divide the class into groups of three or four. Each group opens a dictionary at a page they find interesting and studies the page for a minute or so.

2 Ask them to copy a noughts and crosses grid (3 x 3 squares) on to a piece of paper and put nine different words from the page into the boxes, one into each box.

3 The groups swap completed grids. They now use their dictionaries to compose questions or prompts for which the nine words are the answers. These can be direct questions such as *Where do you see films?* or gap-fills such as *He went to the . . . to see the latest film.* They can include pictures, opposites, or translations. Make sure the questions are not in the same order as the nine words in the grid.

4 The groups pass the grids and questions to another group, who match questions and answers without using dictionaries. They should discuss the questions and work by consensus, not just guesswork.

5 Use dictionaries to check the answers.

VARIATION   The nine words could also come from recent homework or class activities—this then becomes a revision activity.

3.9 Words that go together

LEVEL	**Elementary and above**
TIME	**20 minutes +**
AIMS	**To raise awareness of *collocations*; to encourage students to learn words in combinations rather than as single items.**
MATERIALS	A worksheet for each student; a dictionary for each pair.
PREPARATION	Make a copy of the 'Words that go together' worksheet for each student or prepare a similar one appropriate for your students.
PROCEDURE	1 Give out copies of the worksheet and ask the students to complete it in pairs. 2 Go through the answers (see the key at the end of the chapter on page 90). Ask which answers they found in the dictionary, and where—under the noun or the adjective, or both?
FOLLOW-UP 1	Ask the students how many combinations can be translated directly into their own language(s).
FOLLOW-UP 2	Encourage the class to record new words in a collocation in their vocabulary books.

WORDS THAT GO TOGETHER
Elementary

Match an adjective from list A with a noun from list B to make a logical combination. How many combinations can you make? (You can use the words more than once.)

A		B	
rainy	right	coffee	fruit
Happy	best	language	Christmas
expensive	foreign	day	present
black	fresh	answer	friend

Are any combinations in your dictionary?

Which examples are given for the adjectives and nouns in your dictionary?

Photocopiable © Oxford University Press

WORDS THAT GO TOGETHER

Intermediate

1 Match an adjective from list A with a noun from list B to make a logical combination. How many combinations can you make? (You can use the words more than once.)

A close   cold   milky   mild   free   good   long

B hair   memory   country   curry   weather   coffee   friend

Which combinations are in your dictionary?

What examples are given in your dictionary using the adjectives and nouns above?

2 Which of the adjectives below can be the opposite of the adjectives in a–j?

weak light low serious heavy dim tall runny thin long thick

a thick soup
b strong tea
c light clothes
d high prices

e light rain
f dark trousers
g slight problem

h bright light
i short holiday
j short people

Photocopiable © Oxford University Press

3.10 More than one meaning

LEVEL

Elementary to intermediate

TIME

25 minutes +

AIMS

To raise awareness of common words which function as different parts of speech and which have more than one meaning; to help students find the right meaning of a word.

MATERIALS

A class set of dictionaries; a worksheet for each student.

PREPARATION

Make copies of the 'More than one meaning' worksheet, or create a similar one at an appropriate level.

PROCEDURE

1 Give a copy of the worksheet to each student and ask them to do part A and compare their answers with a partner before starting part B. (See page 91 for an answer key.)

2 They complete part B in pairs, checking in their dictionaries.

3 Give the class a couple of minutes to brainstorm other words with more than one meaning. They can use the dictionary. Write the suggestions on the board.

4 In pairs, the students write 5–10 sentences like those in part B, leaving a gap for the key words. The pairs swap sentences and try to fill the gaps.

5 Return the answers to the original pairs for correction.

FOLLOW-UP

Next lesson, put the class into fours and ask each group to select a letter of the alphabet (perhaps not X, Y, and Z). Give them ten minutes to look through the entries in their dictionary for that letter, making a note of ten words with more than one meaning (**homonyms**). If there are more than ten, they must decide which ones they think are most common. Then ask them to add one more word, but which only has one meaning in the dictionary, and then write their 11 words on the board. When each group has written up their list, give the class ten minutes to try to find which word in each list has only one meaning.

MORE THAN ONE MEANING

Elementary

A Look up the underlined words in a dictionary. Sometimes words which look the same have several completely different meanings. Which meanings given in the dictionary fit the uses of the words here?

1 What's the name of the <u>book</u> you're reading?

2 We took the <u>train</u> to London, but it was expensive.

3 The weather's too nice to stay inside and <u>watch</u> television all day.

4 They've just bought a <u>flat</u> near the city centre.

5 What's your number? I'll give you a <u>ring</u> tonight.

6 I was in bed with a <u>cold</u> for two days.

7 We're going to see a <u>play</u> by a new author next week.

8 No sugar, thanks. I don't like <u>sweet</u> drinks.

B Now complete these sentences using the underlined words from the eight sentences above.

a It's really _____ of you to offer to take us to the station.

b I think my _____ is fast. Have you got the right time?

c It's a popular place. I think it's a good idea to _____ in advance.

d They're professionals. They have to _____ every day.

e They say that Holland is a _____ country.

f Please put your toys away after you _____ with them.

g He bought her a diamond _____.

h The coffee has gone _____. Could I have another?

Photocopiable © Oxford University Press

3.11 Multi-meaning bluff

LEVEL · **Intermediate and above**

TIME · **40–60 minutes**

AIMS · **To raise awareness of *homonyms*.**

MATERIALS · Worksheet and dictionaries for each pair of students.

PREPARATION · Make a copy of the 'Homonyms' worksheet A and B for each group of four learners.

PROCEDURE

1 Ask the class what *back* means. Elicit as many meanings as you can—*my back hurts, the back garden, put a book back, I'm backing Mr Jones*. Explain that these are homonyms—and there are many of them in English. Get the students to look at the various entries for *back* in their dictionaries to see how homonyms are presented. In many dictionaries they are numbered, for example, see^1, see^2, etc.

2 Divide the class into pairs, and give each pair a homonyms worksheet.

HOMONYMS   A

Look up these words in your dictionary and find at least two different meanings for each. Then invent one wholly wrong definition for each word: perhaps you can borrow a definition from another word on the same page.

1 arm   **2** bank   **3** deal   **4** leave

HOMONYMS   B

Look up these words in your dictionary to find at least two different meanings for each.

For each word, invent one wholly wrong definition: perhaps you can borrow a definition from another word on the same page.

1 bolt   **2** case   **3** fine   **4** order

---

3 Each pair checks the meanings of their four words, and invents one untrue meaning for each homonym. When everyone is ready, put each pair against another and explain the game: they have to take turns to define the words. The aim of the game is for the listeners to spot the untrue definition. Award one point for each correct guess.

Example
> Student A: *bore* means to make someone lose interest and
> become tired.
> Student B: *bore* also means to make a small hole in
> something.
> Student A: *bore* is also a word meaning a division of a large
> town (thinking of *borough*).

FOLLOW-UP

Ask the pairs to flick through their dictionaries to find 10–20
more examples of homonyms and distractors for the next game.

Acknowledgements
This is a version of the popular *Call My Bluff* television game.

3.12 Which example?

LEVEL

All

TIME

10 minutes

AIMS

**To familiarize students with examples in dictionaries; to
introduce or revise vocabulary.**

MATERIALS

A list of examples and a dictionary for each pair of students.

PREPARATION

Choose 5–10 words you would like the class to concentrate on:
perhaps new words, words that have caused problems in the past,
or words you would like your students to use more actively. Copy
out the example sentences given in the dictionary for each word
on to a worksheet and make a copy for each student. (There is a
sample worksheet on page 86; the answers are on page 91.)

PROCEDURE

1 Give out the worksheets. Explain what you have done and ask
why dictionaries have such sentences, and whether the students
find them useful or not when they are looking up words.

2 Ask the students to work in pairs. Can they guess which word
each example is supposed to illustrate?

3 They check their dictionaries to see if they were right. If not,
can they think of clearer, more useful example sentences?

WHICH EXAMPLE?
Intermediate

Read these sentences carefully and decide which word is being explained.

1 She's still hesitating about whether to accept the job or not.
2 He was willing to make any sacrifice in order to succeed.
3 Children shouldn't be left on their own.
4 They ignored me and continued their conversation.
5 The course provides a good balance between academic and practical work.
6 We had steak followed by fresh fruit.
7 I've only asked a few friends to the party.
8 He left the job for a combination of reasons.

(Examples from the *Oxford Wordpower Dictionary*)

Photocopiable © Oxford University Press

3.13 Talking sense

LEVEL

Elementary and above

TIME

15–20 minutes

AIMS

To practise skimming skills; to help learners associate words with their five senses; to provide memory training.

MATERIALS

One dictionary per three students.

PROCEDURE

1 Elicit from the class the five senses (i.e. sight, taste, touch, smell, and hearing) and get an example of a particular association for each sense. For example:

   apples and the sense of taste   the sea and hearing

2 Divide the class into groups of three, each with a dictionary. Ask each group to choose a letter of the alphabet to work with. Write *sight taste touch smell hearing* on the board. Explain that for each sense they must find at least four examples of words that can be associated with it, all beginning with their chosen letter. They can refer to the dictionary.

3 Which group found the most associations? Was any sense particularly easy or difficult to find? Why? This will often reflect the students' own preferences and can lead to interesting insights.

4 Make new groups with each person from a different team if possible. Can they remember the words associated with each

sense? This is also a revealing moment: memory tends to favour certain associations, often the more visual, concrete ones. Is that the case? Can they think of ways of recording the words in their vocabulary books that will make use of these sense associations?

5 Tell the class you will repeat the activity again, with different letters, in another lesson. The second time round, memory is often enhanced.

VARIATION

The whole class works from the same page—the challenge is to be the first group to associate all the headwords on the page with the different senses. When finished, groups compare and justify their associations.

3.14 Personalized pages

LEVEL

All

TIME

40 minutes

AIMS

To encourage thinking about the 'usefulness' of words; to encourage discussion.

MATERIALS

A dictionary for each group of three learners

PROCEDURE

1 Divide the class into groups of three, and ask each group to find an interesting page of the dictionary. How many words do they know on the page? Which is the most useful word on the page? What is their understanding of 'useful'? Do all the groups have the same idea? Some examples might be 'I use this word every day' or 'It's a common word in my profession'.

2 Ask the groups to rank the headwords in order of usefulness. All the members of a group must agree—this encourages discussion and **peer teaching**.

3 One person from each group writes the new list of words on the board or an overhead transparency. The rest of the class now ask for explanations of unfamiliar words and ask the group to justify the reasons for their chosen order. Make sure the pace is snappy: you can give each team a 2–3-minute time limit.

4 The teams vote on the ten most useful words from the entire selection on the board.

5 Take feedback: do all the groups agree? If not, why not?

VARIATION

In large classes, rather than calling a member of each team to the board in step 3, ask the groups to stick their lists up on a board. Everyone copies at least two lists. For homework they look through the words and see if they agree with the order of usefulness.

3.15 Collapsing a page

LEVEL

Lower-intermediate and above

TIME

15–20 minutes

AIMS

To focus on the structure and function of words; to encourage vocabulary learning by association.

MATERIALS

A dictionary for every 2–3 students.

PROCEDURE

1 Divide the class into pairs or small groups, each with a dictionary. Ask them to open the dictionary at random and find a page with about 10–15 **headwords**. Make sure each group is working on a different page.

2 Tell students to pair up as many of the words on their page as they can, using any justification, but without using the same word twice. For example:

- two verbs
- two irregular plurals
- two phrasal verbs
- two words that describe clothing

The only relation not allowed is 'beginning with the same letter'!

Examples
Hit and *hitch* can both be used as verbs and nouns.
A *historian* studies *history.*
Hoarse and *hiss* are both to do with speaking.
Finding a *hoard* of treasure can be a *historic* occasion.
Hitherto and *historical* are both to do with the past.

(from the *Oxford Wordpower Dictionary*, p. 305)

3 After five minutes, ask the class to stop and see who has the fewest headwords left over. If one pair finishes before five minutes are up, they can shout 'Stop!' Each group should keep a record of how many words they had left over.

4 The students pass their pages on to the next group or pair, who must try to do better.

VARIATION

1 The whole class works on the same page. Each group keeps a record of their pairings, but not the reason for them.

2 After five minutes, put two groups together and tell them to swap their lists of pairs. The groups justify their lists.

FOLLOW-UP

Tell the groups to close their dictionaries and give them three minutes to recall as many of the pairings as possible.

3.16 Arguing for words

LEVEL

Upper-intermediate and above

TIME

30–40 minutes

AIMS

To encourage discussion; to provide memory training; to help learners create associations as a means of learning vocabulary.

MATERIALS

One dictionary for each group of three.

PROCEDURE

1 Divide the class into groups of three. Each group must choose a topic they are all interested in. This should be quite specific: for example, 'team sports' is better than 'sport'. Give them a minute or so to negotiate a topic, and try to make sure that each group nominates a different topic. Write the topics on the board.

2 Give each group a dictionary—if possible the same edition. Choose at random a page which has 10–15 headwords. Each group works from the same single page. The groups have five minutes to read through the headwords and check the meanings. Circulate and give any help needed.

3 Explain that they are going to try to 'win' words by arguing that as many headwords as possible naturally 'belong' to their chosen topic. Allow 10 minutes for the groups to think up their justifications. This generates a lot of discussion. Warn more advanced groups to anticipate the claims made by other groups, and tell them to try to go one better. Typical comments could be:

Team sports group: 'Hop' is definitely our word—in football we often have to hop as part of our training; young spectators might hop while waiting to get in and see a match.

Rock music group: No, 'hop' is our word—singers and musicians often hop rather than actually dance when they are on stage; there's also a dance where you hop with your partner . . .

4 The groups argue for the words. Set a 30-second time limit for each group's argument for each word. The groups which don't have the floor must listen, but of course they don't have to agree with what they hear. You decide which team deserves to 'win' the word.

5 As a surprise finale, and to reinforce memorization of the words, explain that the team with the most words has to write a 1,000-word composition using the words they have won. When they react—and it will probably be somewhat negative—add that, if they want, they can get rid of the words by producing

counter-arguments in favour of other teams owning the words. This starts what can be a frantic argument with teams trying to offload their words, and is a nice non-competitive way to end the activity.

VARIATION 1

This technique can be used with new vocabulary that you are going to focus on later. The groups choose their topics, then you put the chosen vocabulary items on the board or overhead transparency and ask the groups to check what they mean, and see how they could use the words in connection with their own topics.

VARIATION 2

Instead of arguing for as many words as possible for their own topic, the groups read through the chosen page and discuss which headwords are easiest to associate with which topic on the board. Then they compare and explain their answers.

Answers

3.2   *birds*: starling, owl, crow, sparrow, hawk, crane
trees: beech, chestnut, walnut, elm, willow, oak
fish: trout, cod, salmon, haddock, tuna, herring
type of housing: bungalow, houseboat, bedsit, mansion, penthouse, semi
flowers: daisy, pansy, daffodil, primrose, carnation, buttercup

3.3   *Advanced*
1 cardiology; 2 bole; 3 sap; 4 foliage; 5 VDU; 6 ROM;
7 hard drive; 8 close-up; 9 sound effects; 10 clapper-board;
11 sautéed; 12 batter; 13 whisk; 14 constituency;
15 the cabinet; 16 a white paper; 17 gilts; 18 stocks;
19 dividend; 20 sub poena

Lower-intermediate
1 gear; 2 whiskers; 3 kennel; 4 half-time; 5 track; 6 migraine;
7 temperature; 8 monitor; 9 modem; 10 trailer

3.6   *Elementary*
True: 1, 4, 7, 8, 10

Intermediate
True: 2, 5, 6, 7, 10

Advanced
True: 2, 4, 7, 8, 10

3.9   These are the most likely combinations:

Elementary
foreign language or friend; best friend, present, or answer; fresh food or coffee; Happy Christmas; expensive present, day, Christmas, or coffee; right answer, day, language; black coffee; rainy day or rainy Christmas.

Intermediate

1 close friend—not close weather; but we do say *it's very close today*; cold coffee or weather; milky coffee; mild curry or weather; free country, curry, coffee, or memory; good memory, weather, friend, coffee, or curry; good hair or—possible country; long hair or memory.

2 thin or runny soup; weak tea; heavy clothes; low prices; heavy rain; light trousers; serious problem; dim, weak, or low light; long holiday; tall people.

3.10 **a** sweet; **b** watch; **c** book or ring; **d** train; **e** flat; **f** play; **g** ring; **h** cold

3.12 hesitate, sacrifice, should, continue, balance, follow, only, combination

4 Vocabulary development

Many people believe that learning vocabulary is a question of learning how to organize it in a meaningful way. The activities here invite students to organize vocabulary in several different ways, including by spatial connection (as in 4.1, 'Words of the week'), by topics and themes (as in 4.2, 'Topic Vocabulary', page 95), and by structure (4.11, 'A bit of vocabulary', page 109). This will encourage students to discover their own preferred strategy. Common to all these is the notion of a system which makes learning memorable.

Often the meaning of a word is closely linked to a particular context. Dictionaries give information about using words appropriately. Some words are better in an informal situation, others are dated or even offensive. Many are more often heard, for example, in America or Australia than in the UK. 4.6, 'Who's talking?' (page 100) and 4.7, 'Words and feelings' (page 102) practise finding information about this often delicate area. Another problem is learning the figurative meanings of common nouns, which is practised in 4.12, 'On edge with word fields' (page 111) and 4.13, 'Body language' (page 113).

Later activities encourage students to learn by discovery and intuition (for example, 4.17, 'Unravel an idiom', page 119) and raise students' awareness of how and where to look up idiomatic expressions in the dictionary.

4.1 Words of the week

LEVEL	**All**
TIME	**10 + minutes a day, ongoing through the week.**
AIMS	**To encourage visual memory and association.**
MATERIALS	Large piece of paper for a chart; strips of paper for definitions; class set of dictionaries.
PREPARATION	Make a wall-chart from the piece of paper with the days of the week at the top of five columns. Prepare a strip of paper for each new word.

PROCEDURE

1 Explain that you are doing a vocabulary wall-chart for the week as a project, and show the chart with the days of the week. Continue the lesson as normal, but just before the end of the lesson, ask the students to write every word or expression that has been looked up in a dictionary or taught or discussed into the column for that day.

2 Ask the class to write out explanations, translations, contexts or diagrams illustrating the meaning of each new word on a strip of paper, using the dictionary for help. This can be done for homework. They should organize who is going to write what first: this will help the memory process and will avoid cluttering the walls with dozens of duplicated words and definitions.

3 Next lesson, the students stick their strips of paper on the wall anywhere around the room except on or near the wall-chart. Tell them to keep a note of the words they look up *outside* the class too, and to deal with them in the same way.

4 Continue throughout the week, adding new words to the wall-chart, and getting the students to write or draw the meanings of new words on slips of paper. Remind the students to look at the chart and the meaning slips every day, before and after class. On Friday—or the last of the series of lessons—ask the students to walk around the class picking up an equal number of 'meaning' slips each. The number will depend on how much vocabulary you have covered.

5 The students stick their 'meaning' slips at the bottom of the column where the original vocabulary item is. This can generate useful self-correction—encourage discussion where there is uncertainty. Let them consult a dictionary if there are any problems.

6 Go through the lists to check that there are no lingering problems. Now ask the students to go round the class in pairs, seeing if they can remember which meaning slips were where. They are often surprised by the results.

VARIATION

A second possible memory check is to divide the class into pairs or small groups and ask each group to see if they can remember all the words for a specific day. If you do both techniques, take feedback to see which was most helpful for the learners.

Example of finished wallchart

Monday	Tuesday	Wednesday	Thursday	Friday
catch some red-handed	– noble	– scarce	legal tender.	the final stretch
don't look a gifthorn in the mouth	– worthless/priceless	– dotted	mobility	for days on end
laconic	– run riot	– scattered	luscious	squalid
run for it	– cockroach-infested	– clamber	clubbable	it stands out in my mind
run short	– Mere tourist	– clank	make one's way	heads or tails
run out of	– Sparsely populated areas	– paupers	notable	look like a drowned rat
born and bred	invaluable	– grim	emerge	disinterested
catch some eye	an area with very few inhabitants	– abhorrent	~~pauper~~	with minutes to spare
The police arrested the moment when the boy stole something in a shop	The crowd was completely uncontrollable.	He killed 3 children. It was an ...... crime.	Mark my words	days after days
You haven't got any sugar at home	S.th not valuable at all	The police charged and the crowd split up quickly	rich and delicious food is ___.	nearly home :
someone who doesn't speak too much	I'm a professional traveller, you're just a ___	Prush gone to do s.th. or wake some up	with one important exception	a dirty, filthy place
We don't have enough Try and escape	very high-class people with titles: Lords, Earls, Dukes etc	In the desert water is ...	a form of legal currency	To Toss a coin, To decide something.
try to catch someone/something	full of insects	In England the weather is miserable and ...	to appear	I'll never forget
whom and grew up in a certain place		The old train was making such a terrible noise!	• Just listen to me; to what I say; this is going to come true.	– I was soaking wet.
			walk on the platform to the train	a referee should always be ...

4.2 Topic vocabulary

LEVEL **Elementary and above**

TIME **45 minutes**

AIMS **Reading for gist; vocabulary development; spelling.**

MATERIALS A copy of the grid for each student; dice; a class set of dictionaries.

PREPARATION
1 Prepare a grid with 9 or 12 squares. Either decide on the topic areas you want the students to work on or allow them to choose topics which interest them (or choose some and let them choose the rest).
2 Either make a copy of the grid for each student or get them to make their own in class (see the example overleaf).

PROCEDURE
1 Explain that the students are going to look through the dictionary for words associated with certain topics. Give out the worksheet or ask the students to draw one.
2 If you have left some boxes blank, invite the students to add topic areas in which they are interested. Choose one letter of the alphabet and tell the students that they have to find words beginning with that letter associated with each topic. At elementary level, one word for each is sufficient. For intermediate groups, insist on three or more words. At advanced level, you could decide by chance: bring along a dice and roll it for each box—the students then have to find that number of words for that particular box. The rules are that every word must be in the dictionary, and every word must be spelled correctly (you might also like to insist that at least one must be a new word).
3 Give the class 20–30 minutes to browse through their dictionaries. It doesn't matter if they use different dictionaries. Circulate and check their answers as they go.
4 When they have finished, ask them to compare their answers in groups of four. Any new words must be explained to the rest of the group. How many different words do they have for each topic altogether?
5 Go over the answers with the whole class. Which topics were the most difficult to find words for?

Example with pre-chosen topic areas:

animals	transport	people and professions
things to eat or drink	buildings	activities
things to wear	shapes and sizes	colours
music	plants	emotions

4.3 Themes and topics

LEVEL
All

TIME
20–30 minutes

AIMS
Organizing vocabulary by topics, vocabulary development.

MATERIALS
A topic sheet and a dictionary for each pair.

PREPARATION
Copy the topic sheet, or make one at a suitable level for your students.

PROCEDURE
1 Put the students in pairs and give each pair a copy of the worksheet.
2 The pairs check their answers in fours and see if they agree. (See the end of the chapter, page 124, for an answer key.)
3 Each pair adds a word to at least two of the lists. Allow a few minutes. When they have finished, ask all the pairs to circulate and compare their answers. They add all the new answers to their lists.

COMMENTS
This is a confidence-building way of developing vocabulary as well as team-teaching.

TOPICS

Beginners

Look at these words in your dictionary, then put them in five logical lists.

summer	plane	jeans	golf	student
ferry	shirt	jogging	nurse	autumn
dress	swimming	actor	winter	taxi
football	policeman	spring	skirt	basketball
teacher	car	waiter	belt	bus

	List A	List B	List C	List D	List E
1					
2					
3					
4					
5					
6					

Which list is the shortest? Why?
Can you add two more words to two of the lists?

Photocopiable © Oxford University Press

VARIATION

With monolingual groups, the pairs can add to their lists in their own language, then swap lists and find the translations for each others' words.

4.4 Imaginable adjectives

LEVEL

Elementary and above

TIME

30 + minutes

AIMS

Vocabulary building, to encourage deductions about vocabulary, using dictionaries to confirm guesses, question formation, sensitizing students to common adjective endings.

MATERIALS

A dictionary for each pair.

PREPARATION

Make a list of 10–15 new adjectives that fit in with a current class topic, and think of sample sentences and situations using each one in context.

PROCEDURE

1 Write up on the board or overhead projector a group of 10–15 adjectives you want the class to learn, and ask the class what

they all have in common. Elicit that they are adjectives. Explain that many adjectives have tell-tale endings like *-ous* (for example, *enormous, generous*), *-ible* or *-able* (*horrible, comfortable*), *-al* or *-ial* (*final, essential*), *-ic* (*poetic, dramatic*).

2 Explain that you want everyone to use their feelings, intuition and imagination to decide if each one sounds positive or negative. The students compare answers in pairs. Do not allow them to use dictionaries at this stage.

3 Still using their imaginations, the pairs discuss which adjectives might describe people, places, and objects or situations. Allow a maximum of five minutes.

4 Explain that you want the class to guess the meaning of the words. You are going to use the word in context, and they must ask you questions. Answer their questions in as much detail as you can naturally, without being too explicit. For elementary levels this is a good practice opportunity for question forms. You may want to give the students time to think of suitable questions.

Example

Teacher: I knew a man who was really *aggressive*.
Student: Was he a . . . (teacher, policemen, or singer?)
Teacher: No, he was a businessman, but I don't think the job made him aggressive, it was his character, I think.
Student: Why was he aggressive?
Teacher: I don't know. Perhaps he couldn't control his temper very well.
Student: When was he aggressive?
Teacher: He wasn't always aggressive. Perhaps when was tired.
Student: What did he do then?
Teacher: Well, sometimes he would shout at us, or things like that.

The questions can be open or closed, and the students can ask any questions they like, but try to keep the pace quick. You can tell a little anecdote to illustrate the adjective in context, but be natural. After three or four questions, signal that that's enough and ask students to write down what they think the word means—in their own language if they want—and move on to the next adjective. You may want to give the students time to think of suitable questions, especially at lower levels.

5 Give out dictionaries and ask the pairs to see if their guesses were accurate.

6 How well did they do? What helped them guess the meanings and what confused them?

COMMENTS

Sometimes students are tempted to give up altogether when they come across a new word in a text, or they are thrown when they hear one in conversation. This activity helps develop useful coping strategies.

4.5 At home in the dictionary

LEVEL	**Intermediate and above**
TIME	**20–30 minutes**
AIMS	**To practise reading skills; to encourage cultural insights in mixed national groups; to raise awareness of encyclopedic information in dictionaries; to discuss national stereotypes.**
MATERIALS	A dictionary for each pair.

PROCEDURE

1 Ask the students to suggest people, places, objects, food, or hobbies etc. that are particularly British (or American, Australian, or Irish according to where you are teaching and the interests of the students). Write suggestions on the board, then ask the class to predict which will be in the dictionary, and why. Examples:

   bowler hat, milkman, pub, outback, motel, limousine, cricket, kilt, tartan, crumpet, baseball

2 In pairs, the students check to see how many they can find. Discuss the findings, and the amount of cultural information in a dictionary.

3 Tell the students they are going to look for similar entries about their cultures and countries, or those they are familiar with. Elicit what they might hope or expect to find. On the board write:

Object or clothing	Food or drink	Person or place	Sport or hobbies	Music

   The students skim through the dictionary for five minutes looking for examples for each heading—and others, if they can think of them. Examples from the *Cambridge International Dictionary of English* include:

	Object or clothing	Food or drink	Person or place	Sport or hobbies	Music
Japan	kimono	sushi	geisha	sumo, karate or origami	karaoke
Latin America	sombrero	tortilla	gaucho	siesta	tango or salsa
France	beret	canapé or crudités	boulevard or café	boules	can-can

4 Ask the students to compare their findings. Did they find that one particular type of entry was dominant, such as food types or musical expressions? Which one and why? To what extent do the entries found reflect national stereotypes?

5 Put the students in groups of four or five. If you have a multinational class, make sure the groups are of mixed nationality, and ask the students to compile a chart with all of

the foreign words. Each student explains to the others what the words from their culture mean.

6 In their groups, the students discuss words from their culture(s) that could be added to the dictionary and explain why.

VARIATION 1

In multinational classes, students work in national groups throughout. After step 5 the whole class circulates to compare what has been found for the other cultures.

VARIATION 2

In monolingual classes, put the students into groups and ask each group to look for a certain category—for example, food or clothing—or introduce a competitive element by asking which group can find the most words.

COMMENTS

A word of caution: this activity needs to be handled carefully to avoid national slurs and what could be delicate topics—civil wars, political corruption, insults, etc.

4.6 Who's talking?

LEVEL

Elementary and above

TIME

15 minutes +

AIMS

To develop awareness of different world Englishes and how they are shown in the dictionary; vocabulary differences between US and UK English.

MATERIALS

A dictionary and a copy of the 'Who's talking?' worksheet for each pair.

PROCEDURE

1 Ask the students how they can tell if they are talking to an American, an Englishman, a Scot, or an Australian. Take feedback.

2 Give out copies of the 'Who's talking?' worksheet and ask the students to work through it in pairs. Point out that many dictionaries cross-reference terms in British and American English.

3 Ask them to check the answers in the dictionary, and take feedback (there is an answer key at the end of this chapter, page 125). How many examples depend on spelling (for example, *centre/center*)? Can they think of any other examples that could be different in UK and US spelling? (*-our/-or* words like *colo(u)r, favo(u)r, harbo(u)r*; *-re/er* words like *theatre/er, litre/er*; *-ogue/-og* words like *catalog, dialogue*, in particular.)

WHO'S TALKING?

The words in *italics* in each sentence are especially common in American or British English. Before you look at the dictionary, try to guess who is speaking, and then find the equivalent term in American or British English.

British English   **American English**

1 He's just bought an *apartment*.

2 Are you going *downtown*?

3 I can't eat *sweets*.

4 I need a *vacation*.

5 There was a man lying on the *pavement*.

6 Have you seen the new Spielberg *movie*?

7 We used to go to the *pictures* every week.

8 Where did you go on *holiday* last year?

9 Do you want salt with your *French fries*?

10 What's your favourite *color*?

11 The car's run out of *gas*.

12 I used to live in a *flat* near here.

13 Do you want a lift to the city *centre*?

14 Take the *elevator* to the tenth floor, and your room is on the right.

15 You can't go to an interview wearing those *pants*.

16 *Write me* before you go.

17 They're complaining about the number of *lorries* that use the road.

18 Would you like another *candy bar*?

19 We'll be here Monday *through* Friday.

20 I'm sorry, I haven't got any change, I've only got *notes*.

FOLLOW-UP

You can make a nice visual display of the differences between UK and US English (and other varieties) by putting up large sheets of coloured paper on two walls of the class—one representing UK English and the other US English. Divide the class into two and make each half responsible for one language variety. How many pictures of things associated with that country, and how many words, meanings, or spellings particular to that country, can they put up on their respective pages by the end of the week?

4.7 Words and feelings

LEVEL

Intermediate and above

TIME

45 minutes +

AIMS

To give practice with positive and negative connotations, working with codes such as (derog.)

MATERIALS

A copy of the worksheet for each student; one dictionary per pair or group.

PREPARATION

Copy the worksheet for each student or prepare a similar one suitable for your students.

PROCEDURE

1 Distribute the worksheet to the students and ask them to work in pairs or small groups.

2 Tell the students that many words tell you something about the speaker's attitude to the person or object he or she is describing as well as about what is being described. For example, *fat* sounds negative (although some people say it is neutral). *Well-built* has a more positive ring. Tell half the groups to study the word 'fat', the other half 'thin'.

3 They have ten minutes to decide whether the words at the bottom of the worksheet are positive or negative, using dictionaries for reference. Some words may generate discussion—*chubby* and *slight*, for example. Encourage this.

4 Ask pairs or groups who worked on the same words to compare answers and iron out any disagreements. Next they should try to guess, without using dictionaries, whether the words of the other group are positive or negative (so that the 'fat' groups now guess 'thin' words, and vice versa).

5 Ask the groups to check each others' answers, and explain any difficulties (see the answer key at the end of the chapter, page 125).

Example: Advanced level

FAT	THIN
Positive	Positive
Negative	Negative
fat bloated podgy chubby stout portly thick-set corpulent stocky plump cuddly tubby overweight squat	thin slender scrawny slim bony emaciated gaunt lean skinny gangling weedy slight sveltel anky

FOLLOW-UP   Ask the students to suggest other categories where they would expect to find positive and negative descriptions (for example, beauty—plainness—ugliness; wealth—poverty; generous—careful with money—skinflint; intelligence—ignorance; modern—trendy—old-fashioned). For homework, ask everyone to produce a similar worksheet, which they can compare with their partner's in the next lesson.

4.8 Find the family

LEVEL   **Elementary to intermediate**

TIME   **20–30 minutes**

AIMS   **To encourage students to make associations between words; vocabulary development.**

MATERIALS   A copy of worksheets A, B, and C and one dictionary for each group of three.

PREPARATION   Make copies of the worksheets (or similar ones suitable for your students).

PROCEDURE   1 Divide the class into groups of three. Give each group either worksheet A, B, or C. Explain that they have to find the connections between the words on their worksheets. The similarities might concern grammar, the sound of the words, the meaning, the spelling, and so on.

2 In their groups, the students check the words in their dictionaries and discuss what the words have in common. Then they add a word to each list and pass the worksheet on to the next group.

3 Each group discusses why the new words were added by the previous group. Again, they can check in a dictionary. Then they add another word to each list and pass the worksheet back to the original group.

4 The original groups now check to see if the words which have been added match the criteria they had first thought of. If not, they explain why not.

5 Form new groups of three with one person each from groups A, B, and C. They compare notes and explain their reasoning. (For an answer key see the end of the chapter, page 125.)

FIND THE FAMILY   A

Elementary

Look at these words in your dictionary and see what they have in common. Then add one more word to each list:

1 drum   bass   keyboards   guitar

2 go   drink   eat   drive

3 man   can   pan   hand

4 body   city   lorry   cherry

FIND THE FAMILY   B

Elementary

Look at these words in your dictionary and see what they have in common. Then add one more word to each list.

1 hill   cloud   wind   storm

2 scooter   bike   van   taxi

3 feet   beat   repeat athlete

4 come   find   teach   think

FIND THE FAMILY   C

Elementary

Look at these words in your dictionary and see what they have in common. Then add one more word to each list.

1 over   under   near   by

2 happy   sad   friendly hopeless

3 Thursday   method   path   maths

4 shelf   knife   wife   life

FIND THE FAMILY   A
Intermediate

Look at these words in your dictionary and see what they have in common. Then add one more word to each list.

1 traffic   luggage   toast   news

2 mouse   child   ox   hoof

3 gas   sidewalk   pants   apartment

4 robin   crow   owl   chicken

FIND THE FAMILY   B
Intermediate

Look at these words in your dictionary and see what they have in common. Then add one more word to each list.

1 calf   puppy   foal   lamb

2 barge   judge   hedge   join

3 chap   bike   fiver   photo

4 read   lead   live   bow

FIND THE FAMILY   C
Intermediate

Look at these words in your dictionary and see what they have in common. Then add one more word to each list.

1 depend   rely   pick   live

2 oak   pine   fir   ash

3 hotel   decide   remain   oppose

4 cold   a bus   fire   the post

4.9 Collocation chains

LEVEL	**Intermediate and above**
TIME	**20–30 minutes**
AIMS	**To raise awareness of *collocations*.**
MATERIALS	A worksheet for each student; a dictionary for each pair.
PREPARATION	Make a copy of the 'Collocation chains' worksheet for each student, or make one at a suitable level.

PROCEDURE

1 First read out the following:

fish and ...
salt and ...
(in December) *Merry ...!*

Ask the class to guess what the next word is. How do they know? Explain that there are many fixed (and semi-fixed) expressions like this, and that we call them collocations.

2 Give out the collocation worksheet. Ask the students to work through it in pairs, using a dictionary to confirm their guesses.

3 Go through the answers for the first part (see page 125) and check that everyone understands the various collocations. Then ask the pairs to complete the worksheet by thinking up another five examples of words which have at least four collocates each (this can be done for homework).

4 When the pairs have found their examples—probably with the help of a dictionary—they swap papers with their neighbours and try to find the answers.

COLLOCATION CHAINS

Intermediate

Which word can come after all of the words in these lists to make a common expression? There is a different answer for each line:

1 tea   bed   bath   summer   next   _____

2 cooked   light   square   main   evening   _____

3 busy   week   Christmas   the other   some   _____

4 stone   ground   factory   second   dance   _____

5 direct   internal   international   bumpy   supersonic   _____

6 historic   Victorian   empty   neighbouring   derelict   _____

7 pocket   easy   save   borrow   change   _____

8 blonde   greasy   lose your   body   curly   _____

9 first   foreign   sign   bad   body   _____

10 second   lend a   hour   helping   on   _____

Work with your partner to think of five more words that have several collocations.

a

b

c

d

e

FOLLOW-UP 1   Ask the students to write a short story using at least five of the collocations, but instead of writing the collocations in full, they should just write the first letter of each word, then pass the story on for the next pair to complete.

FOLLOW-UP 2   Hold a class discussion on whether the students think it is a good idea to keep a collocation notebook, or to have a collocation page in their vocabulary book.

FOLLOW-UP 3   See how many collocations the class can collect in a week.

COMMENTS   Learners' monolingual dictionaries are normally a better source of information about collocations than bilingual dictionaries.

4.10 Who's at home?

LEVEL   **Intermediate and above**

TIME   **40–60 minutes**

AIMS   **Vocabulary development; to provide practice with the structure *This is a place where ...***

MATERIALS   A copy of the worksheet for each student; a dictionary for each pair.

PROCEDURE   1 Distribute copies of the worksheet and ask the students to work in pairs. Half the pairs work with the words in list A, the other half with list B.

WHOSE HOME ARE THEY?

Can you divide these words into at least three different groups? What are the groups?

A shed   bowl   cage   den   barracks   vicarage   nest
    hive   wigwam   igloo   villa   manor   motel   stable
    pen   sty   kennel   bungalow

B tenement   mud hut   cottage   camp   monastery
    hostel   penthouse   tent   tank   mansion   cabin
    convent   hall of residence

1

2

3

Others

---

3 Put pairs who worked on A together with pairs who worked on B. They explain the new words to each other, using the structure *This is a place where* … . (Suggestions for categories are given in the answer key at the end of the chapter, page 125.)

4 Ask the students how many they have personally stayed in, and for how long. Then they circulate to find:

– who has stayed in the most different types of 'homes';
– who has stayed in the fewest different types.

5 Make new groups of four and ask each group to choose up to eight words from the list. The groups compose a story or a related series of incidents about 'Staying in unusual places'. The funnier or more unusual, the better. These stories can be written up for homework, and then displayed around the class for the students to read and compare.

COMMENTS

1 Accommodation is a theme which commonly occurs in examinations such as PET, FCE, CAE, or IELTS, so this can be a useful introduction to the theme. The same procedure can be used for any set of related words: jobs, emotions, sports, foods, clothes, animals, hobbies.

2 Making associations between words, or arranging words in groups, is a key memory technique. This is reinforced in steps 4 and 5, which are a crucial part of the activity.

4.11 A bit of vocabulary

LEVEL

Intermediate and above

TIME

30–40 minutes

AIMS

Vocabulary development; to provide practice with a common noun pattern; to sensitize students to information given as cross-references, *idioms*, and examples.

MATERIALS

A copy of worksheets A and B for each student; a dictionary for each pair.

PROCEDURE

1 Give out worksheet A and ask the students to work in pairs and find as many combinations, sayings, or **idioms** as possible that link words from column A with words from column B—for example, *a sense of humour*.

2 Ask them to check their suggestions in the dictionary. Where did they find the answers?

How many were they given as:

– **headwords**
– cross-references
– idioms
– examples in **entries**?

This will vary from dictionary to dictionary. Students need to learn to scan entries for relevant information, and to realize that they can learn useful words and expressions from various parts of a dictionary entry.

3 Give out worksheet B. The students complete the sentences with expressions from worksheet A. There is an answer key at the end of the chapter (page 126).

FOLLOW-UP 1

In pairs, the students produce similar worksheets to A and B, using the other possible combinations they found in step 1 above, and swap their work. This can be done for homework.

FOLLOW-UP 2

Each student adds similar 'noun plus noun' combinations to their vocabulary books throughout the week. At the end of the week, how many different combinations have been found?

A ... OF ...

Upper-intermediate A

Find common expressions by joining one noun from column A with one from column B using 'of'. There may be several possible combinations for some words.

The first example has been done for you:

A sense of humour

Use your dictionary to check your choices:

A	B
1 way	**a** life
2 manner	**b** mouth
3 **sense**	**c** day
4 standard	**d** **humour**
5 matter	**e** fact
6 world	**f** living
7 time	**g** thinking
8 word	**h** speaking
9 mine	**i** difference
10 change	**j** flats
11 run	**k** bad luck
12 block	**l** address
13 mark	**m** information
14 sign	**n** respect

A...OF...

Upper-intermediate **B**

Complete the sentences with expressions from worksheet A.

1 To my _____, £100 for two nights in a London hotel is reasonable.

2 I've had a _____ lately. Everything's been going wrong!

3 I'm writing to let you know of my _____: I've got a new flat.

4 In some cultures young people don't talk in front of their parents as a _____.

5 There's a _____ between borrowing from a friend and getting money from the bank.

6 He lives in that huge _____ in the city centre.

7 I thought there was a party there, but when we arrived there was no _____.

8 You want to know what the capital of Paraguay is? Ask John, he's a _____.

9 Do you think any shops will be open at this _____?

10 The _____ is very high in Japan: everyone has all the latest gadgets!

11 They didn't learn about the concert by advertising—the fans learnt by _____.

12 He works for in the family business so his father is, in a _____, his boss.

13 'Are you English?' 'No, I'm Welsh, as a _____.'

14 People say that the English have a very strange _____.

4.12   On edge with word fields

LEVEL	**Upper-intermediate and above**
TIME	**40–60 minutes**
AIMS	**Vocabulary development; to provide practice with reading skills; to help students distinguish between related words.**
MATERIALS	A copy of the 'Word field' worksheets 1 and 2 for each student; a dictionary for each pair.
PREPARATION	Copy the worksheets, or make similar ones suitable for your students.

PROCEDURE

1 Put the students in pairs and give each student a copy of worksheet 1. Allow 10–15 minutes for them to find all the answers to part A using their dictionaries. Let the pairs check together to see if they have all found the right words.

WORD FIELDS 1

a All the following words are related in some way. Use your dictionary to complete the words.

1 E D _ _   6 V E _ _ E
2 R I _   7 F R _ _ _ E
3 B R _ _ K   8 O U _ _ _ _ _ T S
4 B _ _ M   9 B O _ _ E R
5 M A _ _ _ N   10 B O _ _ _ _ R Y

What do they have in common?

What is the difference between them?

WORD FIELDS 2

Complete the following sentences with words from worksheet 1.

1 The fence at the bottom of the garden marks the _____ between my land and my neighbour's.

2 Careful! I won't be able to lift my glass without spilling if you fill it to the _____.

3 My salary isn't great, but there are good _____ benefits like having a company car and a good canteen.

4 For our last holiday we rented a small house near the _____ of France and Switzerland.

5 Somebody has written notes in the _____ of this book.

6 They live on the _____ of Bristol.

7 We had a quick picnic on the _____ of the road, watching the cars drive by.

8 Excuse me, can I have a new cup? The _____ of this one is chipped.

9 Don't leave those books on the _____ of the desk. Someone will knock them off.

10 They're on the _____ of bankruptcy. The company's probably going to close down.

Can any words be used more than once?

Photocopiable © Oxford University Press

2 Encourage the pairs to debate what the words have in common (the notion of edge or limit) and, more importantly, to check the dictionary to see what differences are suggested between words. Are there any distinctions that are not clear? If so, perhaps using a bilingual dictionary can clarify problems.

3 When everyone is happy with the differences between the words, ask the pairs to work through the second worksheet and compare answers with their neighbours to see if there is a degree of consensus.

4 Check the answers (see the answer key at the end of the chapter, page 126). Which words seem more figurative, and which more concrete?

5 In pairs, the students produce 5–10 questions for other pairs about the uses of the different words, and write them on a piece of paper.

Examples
Can you say 'at the *edge* of midnight'?
Is 'brink' always positive?
What other meaning does 'fringe' have?

The questions can either be genuine questions to which they want to know the answers, or test questions based on what they know or have read.

6 The pairs swap questions and discuss them, referring to their dictionaries when necessary.

7 Return the questions to the original pairs. Take feedback and see if there are any unresolved problems.

COMMENTS

Showing that dictionaries can be a source of information about metaphorical and extended uses of words is important. The gap-fill activity is very traditional—you may prefer to leave it out and concentrate on the discussion stages. Students, however, often appreciate this format, particularly since it often occurs in tests with precisely this type of **word field**. Step 5 could be done as homework and the activity could take place over two or three lessons.

4.13 Body language

LEVEL

Lower-intermediate and above

TIME

20–30 minutes

AIMS

Vocabulary development; to raise awareness of the multiple meanings of words; awareness of figurative uses of concrete nouns.

MATERIALS

A worksheet for each student; a dictionary for each pair.

PREPARATION

Make a copy of the 'Body language' worksheet for each student, or make a similar one at a suitable level for your students.

PROCEDURE

1 Give out the worksheet and ask the students to look through it in pairs. The answers are given for guidance at the foot of the worksheet—but not in the right order. Weaker classes might like to do this as a matching activity. With more advanced classes, ask them to cover up the answers at this stage.

2 The students use a dictionary to find the answers and make a note of any other examples of parts of the body that can be used metaphorically.

3 After ten minutes, put pairs together to compare their findings in groups of four (see the end of this chapter, page 126, for an answer key).

4 Ask the groups to discuss the connections between the situations and the use of parts of the body. For example, *head* has associations with thinking, leading, and being first; *back* gives the idea of being behind, and so on.

5 Feedback: in their language(s), do they use parts of the body in similar expressions to the examples on the worksheet? What about any others?

BODY LANGUAGE
Lower-intermediate

A How many parts of the body can you list in five minutes?

B Choose the right word to complete these sentences.

1 She put her coffee down on the *arm/hand* of the chair.

2 In 1995 he became the *neck/head* of the company.

3 That chair is unstable. I think one of the *arms/legs* is shorter than the others.

4 The second *hand/foot* of my watch has stopped.

5 I found her lying at the *leg/foot* of the stairs. She must have fallen.

6 He put his coat over the *back/shoulder* of the chair.

7 The *heart/head* of the problem in that company is money: the salaries are very low.

8 I need a new comb—this one has a lot of *ears/teeth* missing.

9 One of the special features of Concorde is its strangely shaped *finger/nose*.

10 We stayed in a village at the *hand/foot* of the mountain.

BODY LANGUAGE
Upper-intermediate

A How many parts of the body can you list in five minutes?

B The answer to each of the following questions is a part of the body. Which?

1 My father usually sits at the . . . of the table.

2 What are you doing in this . . . of the woods?

3 He has disappeared from the . . . of the earth. Nobody can find him.

4 Mr Smith has been . . . of the company for two years.

5 Pat's in charge of the European . . . of the company.

6 We used to have boiled eggs with . . . of toast.

7 She found a place at the . . . of the cliff and started sunbathing.

8 The clock . . . is scratched, and the little . . . is bent, but I can repair it for you.

9 Let's toss for it. . . . you win, tails I win.

10 The pilot struggled to get the . . . of the plane up. We thought he was going to crash.

11 The last . . . of my journey from Brazil to Mexico was the most difficult.

12 The climbers were the first to go up the north . . . of the mountain in winter.

13. I love the . . . of a lettuce—it's so crisp.

14 I'm terrible at practical things. I can't even get a thread through the . . . of a needle.

15 He grabbed the bottle by the . . . , ready to use it as a weapon.

16 He was so methodical, he even used to polish the . . . of his shoes.

17 I need a new saw. Many of the . . . of this one are bent.

18 The main . . . of her autobiography deals with her childhood.

19 She sat down, put her coffee on the . . . of the chair, and turned the television on.

20 When I had a puncture on the motorway, I spent two hours waiting on the hard . . .

Helpful hint: these are the answers, but not in the right order:

shoulder head face body neck arm teeth head
nose face legs hand tongue heads face foot
heart eye fingers neck arm

4.14 Animal verbs

LEVEL	**Intermediate and above**
TIME	**20 minutes**
AIMS	**Vocabulary development.**
MATERIALS	A dictionary for every 3–4 students.

PROCEDURE

1 Put the students in groups of three or four and give them five minutes to make a list of as many animals and insects as possible in English.

2 Take feedback. Ask how many of the animal names can be used as verbs, for example *a fish—to fish*. Warn the students that there are many animal verbs in English—but often with a metaphorical meaning. Give them a minute or so to discuss.

3 They check their ideas in their dictionaries, and make a note of any particles or prepositions associated with the animals as verbs—for example, *monkey around*.

4 Were there any surprises? Which animals do not work as verbs? (For example, 'to cat' doesn't, but one can be 'catty'; 'to bee' doesn't exist, but we have the idiom 'busy as a bee'.)

5 Everyone circulates to compare and contrast notes (they may have had different animals on their original lists).

COMMENTS The following are commonly used animal verbs: to dog, snake, fish, worm something out of someone, beaver away, crow, wolf, horse around, ape, monkey around or about, fox, badger, duck, hound, ram, cow, pig, squirrel, bat, chicken out of.

FOLLOW-UP Everyone writes a diary of the day or week using as many animal verbs (and **idioms**) as possible. This can be done as homework.

4.15 *-ful* and *-less*

LEVEL	**Intermediate and above**
TIME	**40 minutes**
AIMS	**Vocabulary building; appreciation of *collocations*.**
MATERIALS	A copy of the worksheet for each student; a dictionary for each pair.

PROCEDURE

1 Give out the worksheets to the students, and ask them to work in pairs to complete the categories without referring to their dictionaries.

2 They check in their dictionaries and make a note of any surprises, then compare answers with their neighbours. (See the answer key on page 126.)

3 Divide the class into groups of four. Each group takes one line of words from the list. They have five minutes to think of at least two nouns that combine with each *-ful* and *-less* adjective, and think of a general context for each.

Example

For the Intermediate worksheet, working with line 2:

thinking of *wonderful*, they choose 'surprise/news'; for *endless*, 'meetings/rain'

4 One representative from each group writes their nouns on the board, in no particular order.

5 The groups discuss which adjectives go with which nouns.

6 Take feedback and discuss any problems.

FOLLOW-UP

The students think up another 10–20 words which could be used in a similar activity using *-ful* and *-less* (*fruit, respect, peer, mother,* etc.), or they create a worksheet for other suffixes: *-ness* and *-ence, -ous* and *-al*.

-FUL AND *-LESS*

Intermediate

Look at the list of word or word-stems below and divide them into three categories:

a Those which only make words with . . . *-ful*
b Those which only make words with . . . *-less*
c Those which make words with both . . . *-ful* and . . .*-less*

thank	grate	meaning	thought	help	tear
wonder	hope	point	end	motion	penny	care
rest	sleep	pain	use	harm	cheer	beauty

-FUL AND *-LESS*

Advanced

Look at the list below and divide the words into three categories:

a Those which make words with . . .*-ful*
b Those which make words with . . .*-less*
c Those which make words with both . . .-ful and . . . *-less*

resent	regard	heart	heed	master	mind	fault
reck	sense	taste	spite	worth	price	delight
truth	waste	dread	charm	mercy	shame	

4.16 Find a proverb or idiom

LEVEL

Intermediate and above

TIME

30–40 minutes

AIMS

Vocabulary development; to practise finding idiomatic expressions in dictionary *entries*.

MATERIALS

A copy of the 'Proverb or idiom finder' worksheet for each student; a dictionary for each pair.

PROCEDURE

1 Divide the class into pairs, and give each student a copy of the worksheet. Ask them to think of a proverb in their own language and to translate it into English.

2 One student from each pair writes one proverb or **idiom** on the board. Discuss the similarities and differences, and check that everyone knows what they mean. In multilingual groups, compare proverbs across cultures: do they have the same ideas, and use the same 'source material' such as animals, time, and so on? See if there are English equivalents that can be compared.

3 The pairs choose the key words that might occur in the proverbs. These should be single words. If they have difficulty at this stage, ask them to translate some of the key words that occur in proverbs in their own languages. You can also remind the class that nature, the world of animals, and parts of the body frequently feature in proverbs and sayings.

4 The students check in their dictionaries to see if their key words occur in English sayings or proverbs. When they find a proverb, they adapt or copy out the example and then add what the meaning or use is.

5 The pairs circulate and compare notes. How many different proverbs did they find? How many proverbs touch on the same theme? What sort of key words were the most and least productive?

FOLLOW-UP

Next lesson ask what the most productive key words were and write them on the board. Now divide the class into fours, and see which foursome can recall the most proverbs without referring back to the proverb finder.

VARIATION

This can be adapted for sayings, idioms, phrasal verbs, and prepositional phrases. It is a very effective memory enhancer.

Example with phrasal verbs

Key word: *make*

Sentence: *Have you made up your mind about which computer to buy?*

Meaning, use: talking about decisions

PROVERB OR IDIOM FINDER		
Key word	**Example**	**Meaning, use**
1 fish	*I was like a fish out of water among those high-class people*	When you feel uncomfortable in a situation because you are not used to it
2		
3		
4		
5		
6		

Photocopiable © Oxford University Press

4.17 Unravel an idiom

LEVEL   Intermediate and above

TIME   20–30 minutes

AIMS   Vocabulary development; help with making guesses about *idioms*.

MATERIALS   A worksheet for each pair of students; a dictionary for each pair.

PREPARATION

Make a copy of the 'Unravel an idiom' worksheet for each student or prepare a similar one suitable for your students.

PROCEDURE

1 Divide the class into pairs and give each pair two copies of the worksheet and a dictionary.

2 The pairs try to guess what the possible idiomatic combinations are before they look them up in the dictionary. Ask the class how to find an idiom in the dictionary. Do they need to look up the first word? If not, which word? (Generally, dictionaries list idioms under the first lexical word, not prepositions, articles, or verbs like *have* and *be*.) For an answer key, see page 126.

3 Once they have worked out the idioms, it is very useful to ask students to think of a context where they could use the idioms naturally. Tell them that you heard all these idioms yesterday—some at home, some on the way to work, some at work, and some when you went out at night. Ask them to imagine which you heard in which situation.

UNRAVEL AN IDIOM

1 Look at the jumble of words below. These are the key words of eight common English idioms. There are two key words given for each idiom. Can you guess which words occur together in the idioms?

greener	cat	fish	water
bag	grass	moon	irons
fire	blue	rock	pull
leg	boat	pay	nose

2 Before you check: what do you think the idioms mean?

3 Now check your guesses in the dictionary and write the idioms here:

a

b

c

d

e

f

g

h

4 While reading, you probably saw other idioms that use some of the key words. Make a similar jumble of key words, and see if your neighbour can match them up.

Photocopiable © Oxford University Press

FOLLOW-UP

Present the same jumble again later in the week and see how well the students remember the idioms. The results are often surprising.

COMMENTS

1 This discovery mode of learning idioms is motivating and memorable.

2 Encouraging students to get a feel for idioms helps when they come across idiomatic language in newspapers—which often have a surprising amount of non-literal language.

4.18 Pairs with prepositions

LEVEL

Intermediate and above

TIME

30–45 minutes

AIMS

To revise verb plus preposition or particle pairs.

MATERIALS

A dictionary for each pair.

PROCEDURE

1 Divide the class into pairs. Ask them to draw two 3 x 3 grids and copy nine common verbs into the squares of one grid, one verb per square as in the example, and on the other grid to put prepositions that go with the verbs in the corresponding squares: for example *go + away*, *bring + back*.

2 Give each pair a dictionary to check that the combinations exist and to make sure that they are happy with the meanings.

3 Collect all the completed grids and put all the verb grids in one pile and all the preposition grids in another. Shuffle each pile and distribute them around the class so that each pair receives one of each.

4 The pairs see how many combinations are possible from the nine verbs and prepositions they have. They can use any verb with any preposition. At each stage they should check with a dictionary and make a note of what they discover.

5 After a couple of minutes, ask the pairs for the total number of possible combinations they have. Keep a score on the board. When you have all the scores, ask the pairs to pass their preposition worksheet to the pair on their left, and explain that the game stops when one pair has found a total of 20–30 possible combinations (choose the target according to the level of your class).

6 Repeat the process, with pairs discussing possible combinations, until one pair reaches the total.

7 Put the pairs together to make fours and ask them to compare the different combinations they found. Which verbs combine with most prepositions? Which prepositions combine with most

verbs? Again, encourage them to check their ideas in a dictionary.

8 Write three topics such as Work, Hobbies, and Travel on the board (according to the class's interests), and ask the groups to find five different verb–preposition combinations that could be used when talking about these topics. Take feedback.

Example

VERB GRID		
work	take	bring
go	make	do
write	read	speak
PREPOSITION GRID		
through	up	back
away	up	with
down	through	up

VARIATIONS   You can use this activity with verbs + adverbs or any other combining form, such as verbs + gerunds or verbs + infinitives without 'to', verbs + infinitives, adjectives + nouns.

4.19 Complete the saying

LEVEL	**Intermediate and above**
TIME	**15–20 minutes**
AIMS	**Vocabulary development, to help with looking up key words in *idioms*.**

MATERIALS

Worksheets A and B; a dictionary for each pair.

PREPARATION

Make copies of the 'Complete the saying' worksheets for everyone to have either A or B, or prepare similar worksheets suitable for your students.

PROCEDURE

1 Put the class into pairs and distribute the worksheets so that each pair has *two* copies of either A or B. Ask the pairs to predict what the missing words could be before looking in a dictionary. Ask them which word they will look up to try to find the answers.

2 Allow the students a few minutes to check in a dictionary.

3 Form new pairs with one person from A working with one person from B. Ask them to check together, see if they found the same answer, and how they found the answers in the dictionary.

4 Ask the students how their dictionary lists idioms and sayings. Which are the most useful words to look up in their dictionaries? (Sometimes the first noun is the key word and sometimes the first adjective, but it varies from dictionary to dictionary. The important thing is for students to learn what their dictionary does.)

FOLLOW-UP

Ask the students to choose five idioms and write a short story—or a sequence of individual sentences—using the sayings in an appropriate context, but with *both* the key words missing. This can be done for homework. Put the stories up around the walls; everyone circulates round the class reading them and adding the words that were missing.

COMPLETE THE SAYING   A

Advanced

How would you complete the following common expressions?

1 Out of sight, out of _____.
2 He knows every trick in the _____.
3 First come, first _____.
4 Come on. Get your act _____.
5 I told him to pull his _____. (two words)
6 You've got to take the rough with the _____.
7 Sorry, I've got a memory like a _____.
8 Cars like that cost an arm and a _____.
9 Where there's a will, there's a _____.
10 If you can't beat them, _____. (two words)

Photocopiable © Oxford University Press

COMPLETE THE SAYING   B

Advanced

How would you complete the following common expressions?

1 Out of _____, out of mind.
2 He knows every _____ in the book.
3 First _____, first served.
4 Come on, get your _____ together.
5 I told him to _____ his socks up.
6 You've got to take the _____ with the smooth.
7 Sorry, I've got a _____ like a sieve.
8 Cars like that cost an _____ and a leg.
9 Where there's a _____, there's a way.
10 If you can't _____, join them. (two words)

Photocopiable © Oxford University Press

Answers

4.3   professions: student, nurse, actor, policeman, waiter, teacher

seasons: summer, autumn, winter, spring

clothing: jeans, shirt, dress, skirt, belt

transport: plane, ferry, taxi, car, bus

hobbies or sports: jogging, golf, swimming, football, basketball

4.6 1 US(flat); **2** US (city centre); **3** UK (candy);
4 US (holiday); **5** UK (sidewalk); **6** US (film);
7 UK (movies); **8** UK (vacation); **9** US (chips);
10 US (colour); **11** US (petrol); **12** UK (apartment);
13 UK (downtown); **14** US (lift); **15** US (trousers);
16 US (write to me); **17** UK (trucks); **18** US (sweet);
19 US (from ... until or to); **20** UK (bills)

4.7 Suggested answers:
Fat   positive: stout, portly, thick-set, stocky, cuddly, plump
neutral to negative: fat
negative: bloated, podgy, chubby, tubby, overweight, squat, corpulent

Thin   positive: slender, slim, slight, svelte
positive to neutral: thin, lean
negative: scrawny, bony, emaciated, gaunt, skinny, gangling, weedy, lanky

4.8 Elementary   **A** **1** instruments; **2** irregular verbs; **3** words with /æ/ sound; **4** form plural in *-ies*.

B **1** form adjectives with y; **2** types of transport; **3** contain the sound /i:/; **4** irregular verbs

C **1** prepositions of place; **2** form nouns with *-ness*; **3** contain /θ/; **4** form plurals with *-ves*

Intermediate   **A** **1** uncountable nouns; **2** have irregular plurals; **3** US English; **4** birds

B **1** words for young animals; **2** contain /dʒ/ sound; **3** informal words; **4** homographs (words with two different meanings and different pronunciations)

C **1** combine with the preposition *on*; **2** trees; **3** stress on second syllable; **4** all collocate with 'catch'

4.9 time, meal, day, floor, flight, building, money, hair, language, hand

4.10 Suggestions:

where animals live	nest, den, hive
where animals are confined	pen, cage, tank, bowl, stable, sty, shed, kennel
for professional groups	vicarage, monastery, barracks, convent, hall of residence
for paying guests	motel, hostel, tent, villa
ethnic dwellings	igloo, wigwam, mud hut
permanent homes	bungalow, tenement, cottage, mansion, penthouse, manor

temporary homes   hall of residence, cabin, tent, camp, villa

4.11 Worksheet A **1** g; **2** h; **3** d; **4** f; **5** e; **6** i; **7** c; **8** b; **9** m; **10** l; **11** k; **12** j; **13** n; **14** a

Worksheet B **1** way of thinking; **2** run of bad luck; **3** change of address; **4** mark of respect; **5** world of difference; **6** block of flats; **7** sign of life; **8** mine of information; **9** time of day; **10** standard of living; **11** word of mouth; **12** manner of speaking; **13** matter of fact; **14** sense of humour

4.12 Worksheet 1 **1** edge; **2** rim; **3** brink; **4** brim; **5** margin; **6** verge; **7** fringe; **8** outskirts; **9** border; **10** boundary

Worksheet 2 **1** boundary; **2** brim; **3** fringe; **4** border; **5** margin; **6** outskirts; **7** verge; **8** rim; **9** edge; **10** brink

Edge could be used in **6**, **7**, and **9**.

4.13 Upper-intermediate **1** head; **2** neck; **3** face; **4** head; **5** arm; **6** fingers; **7** foot; **8** face; hand; **9** heads; **10** nose; **11** leg; **12** face; **13** heart; **14** eye; **15** neck; **16** tongue; **17** teeth; **18** body; **19** arm; **20** shoulder

Lower-intermediate **1** arm; **2** head; **3** legs; **4** hand; **5** foot; **6** back; **7** heart; **8** teeth; **9** nose; **10** foot

4.15 Intermediate **a** grateful, wonderful, beautiful
b penniless, motionless, sleepless, endless, pointless
c thank, meaning, thought, help, hope, care, rest, pain, use, harm, cheer, tear

Advanced **a** resent, master, delight, truth, waste, dread, spite
b regard, heart, fault, reck, sense, worth, price, charm, heed
c mind, taste, mercy, shame

4.17 rock the boat
the grass is always greener on the other side of the fence
once in a blue moon
let the cat out of the bag
have many irons in the fire
like a fish out of water
pull someone's leg
pay through the nose

5 Using texts

This chapter contains 18 activities which focus on using dictionaries while working with texts of different types. The first activities concentrate on comprehension and the composition of texts and suggest ways of working with new vocabulary, including the important question of prioritizing which new words to look up (for example, 5.2, 'Five new words', page 129). Not all new words are equally important to all learners. Students should learn to evaluate the usefulness of what they look up (5.6, 'Would-be vocabulary', page 134).

Texts are not just collections of individual words. Efficient readers have learnt to process texts as **chunks**, meaningful combinations of groups of words. 5.3, 'Colour connections' (page 130) encourages this.

When we talk about texts, all too often we overlook the texts which are most important to students, namely the ones they themselves write. 5.11, 'Weather words and global warming' (page 140), 5.13, 'Writing' (page 142), and 5.14, 'Dictionary dictation' (page 143) use dictionaries to help students in the planning and editing stages of writing.

Other activities exploit texts for **word formation** (for example, 5.15, 'Compound texts', page 143), and grammar practice (5.16, 'Coded prepositions', page 145), while 5.17, 'Fill that gap' (page 146) provides practice in a skill which is often tested in exam questions.

5.1 Peer teaching for texts

LEVEL	**Elementary and above**
TIME	**15–25 minutes**
AIMS	*Peer teaching*; **explaining new vocabulary; to encourage students to take responsibility for learning.**
MATERIALS	Texts for each student (see 'Preparation'); one dictionary per four students.
PREPARATION	1 Find a text at a suitable level with new vocabulary. Travel writing or stories that use descriptive language to create a sense of atmosphere work well (see the example below). At elementary level the text will be quite short—as little as

100–150 words will do. For more advanced classes, find texts up to 1000 words long.

2 Divide the text into four equal sections and number them.

PROCEDURE

1 Give each student a copy of the text you have chosen. They read through it silently to find the three most important facts about the text. No dictionaries at this stage.

2 Put the students in pairs and ask them to compare their three facts. Explain that each pair will be responsible for checking and explaining the vocabulary of one part of the text. Everyone reads it through again, underlining the words or expressions they would like to check.

3 Tell each pair which numbered section they are responsible for. Allow them five minutes for checking everything they think the other members of the class might want to know, using dictionaries.

4 Put the students in groups of four with one person who has looked at each section of the text. Everyone can now ask for help with the meaning of the words underlined earlier, and can explain one part of the text.

Sample text
Intermediate and above

Cities supply the bear essentials

1

CITIES across the American West are being invaded by black bears foraging for food. As the urban sprawl pushes further into the forests and mountain ranges, the bears are turning to civilisation for their sustenance and are becoming a common sight in populated areas.

On the outskirts of Los Angeles bears are often seen foraging in rubbish bins and even cooling off in swimming pools. Recently a bear named Samson became a celebrity after he was filmed lolling in a hot tub. He has now been put in a zoo.

2

The California town of Mammoth Lakes, which has a live-and-let-live policy towards bears, has about 40 living within the city limits. Bears wander the streets, oblivious to traffic, and hang around restaurant rubbish bins. Nine have been killed by cars so far this year. 'What we've done is create a huge wildlife sanctuary with its central food source in the middle of town,' said police chief Michael Donnelly. 'This is a town that wants to get along with nature. It may be naive when it comes to bears but we have set out to live with them at a safe distance.'

The town has appointed a 'bear manager' to deal with the problem. Steve Searles uses pepper spray, exploding flares and rubber bullets to frighten the bears away from houses and rubbish bins.

3

'They're incredibly determined creatures,' he said. 'It's hard to break them of bad habits.'

The animals now recognise Searles and run when they see his vehicle approaching. They thrive on their diet of discarded hamburgers and other cast-off food and some of them now weigh as much as 600lb.

The fat content and calories has also boosted their fertility and instead of having one cub, bears in Mammoth regularly produce two and three offspring each year.

'Some people living here think of the bears as their pets,' said Mr Donnelly. 'One lady refers to them as "my dogs" and puts out 50lb bags of dog food for them.

We're trying to change attitudes like that.'

4

The problem is becoming acute in nearby Yosemite National Park, a popular tourist destination where last week four bears, including a mother with two cubs, were put down because they would not stop breaking into cars and threatening people. Hungry bears have caused £300,000 in damage to parked cars in Yosemite so far this year.

In Colorado 35 bears have been killed in the past two years after blundering on to busy streets or causing damage to property.

'At no time in history have we had as many bears and people living in close quarters,' said Gary Alt, a bear biologist.

(Adapted from the *Daily Telegraph*, 25 Nov. 1997, p.18)

| VARIATION | With smaller classes or shorter texts, you can divide the text into three or even two parts. |

VARIATION

With smaller classes or shorter texts, you can divide the text into three or even two parts.

COMMENTS

This is a well tried and tested activity that generates a lot of peer teaching. It also makes it possible to tackle texts that are longer than normally comfortable at lower levels.

5.2 Five new words

LEVEL

All

TIME

30 minutes +

AIMS

To raise awareness about how to prioritize new vocabulary; to work out meanings from contexts; to develop tolerance for unknown vocabulary.

MATERIALS

A text for each student (see 'Preparation'); one dictionary for each group of three.

PREPARATION

Find a text at a suitable level with 10 + new words or expressions. At higher levels, texts with figurative use of language work well. Make one copy of the text for each student. This task works best with longer texts, for example, articles from newspapers or extracts from works of fiction, perhaps a class reader which the students have not read yet.

PROCEDURE

1 Give each student a copy of the text. They read it through to get a general idea of the topic and to look for something that catches their attention, but they must not use a dictionary yet. Allow 5–10 minutes for this. Examples could be an image, an unusual fact, or new vocabulary.

2 Put students in groups of three and ask them to compare their interpretation of the main ideas. Can they agree on five key facts about the text, still without using a dictionary? What caught their attention?

3 Ask the students to look back through the texts and underline the words or expressions that are new to them, still without dictionaries.

4 Ask the groups to compare what they have underlined, and explain that in a couple of minutes you will allow each group to check exactly five words or expressions in the text. First, they must agree which five words they want to look up. This will encourage them to try to guess the meaning from context and to peer teach one another where possible.

5 One student from each group writes the five words they have chosen on the board. Are there any differences between the groups? If so, does anyone want to change their list of words?

They can make as many changes as they want, as long as they still have a maximum of five words or expressions on their list. Keep the pace brisk.

6 Give each group of three a dictionary. Allow a few minutes for the students to check their chosen words or expressions.

7 Make new groups with each member from a different group. They summarize the text orally, in as much detail as possible. Ask them to evaluate how useful their chosen words were for improving their understanding of the text.

8 Take class feedback. Which of the words on the board (from step 5) proved the most useful for an improved understanding? Which words were not so useful? In general, how can they decide if a word is worth looking up?

VARIATION   The whole class must agree on the five words to be looked up.

5.3 Colour connections

LEVEL   **Elementary and above**

TIME   **30 minutes +**

AIMS   **To associate words in context; to raise awareness of *collocations*; and to show how texts are composed of *chunks* of language.**

MATERIALS   A suitable text; coloured pencils; and a dictionary for each pair.

PREPARATION   Find a text of up to 250 words at a suitable level for the class, containing a number of collocations and 5–10 new words or expressions (see the example on the next page). Texts from authentic sources, particularly magazine stories, or newspaper reports of semi-technical stories like space shuttles, scientific discoveries, or legal cases work well. Make a copy for everyone.

PROCEDURE   1 Distribute the text that you want the students to work on and ask them to read quickly to find the main idea of each paragraph. They discuss it in pairs—no dictionaries yet.

2 Give the pairs at least two different coloured pencils each, and ask them to colour in ten word partnerships they know, for example, 'depend on', 'catch a bus', or 'good morning'. Explain that sometimes partners are not adjacent: *He waited by the phone for a call.*

3 They re-read the text, checking as many new words as they like, but they must always connect each one to some other word or phrase in the text by colour. They must have a justification for the connection—for example, by grammar, logic, or theme.

4 Ask the pairs to check in fours to see what similarities and differences they have.

5 They write out a list of the word groups or 'chunks' they have found, including the new vocabulary, in the order that they appear in the original text.

6 Pairs swap their lists and, without looking back at the original text, use the chunks as a prompt for re-creating the text orally.

VARIATION

Instead of listing the chunks in order in step 5, they could be scattered around a page (or on the board) randomly. In pairs, the students have to recreate the text by sequencing the chunks.

COMMENTS

Students often make a note of individual words when they use a dictionary. However, it helps if they can learn a word in a 'chunk'—either adjective plus noun, or verb plus noun, or verb plus preposition—*He stared open-mouthed in amazement* reinforces 'open-mouthed' better than a simple translation. Not only does this help with contextualizing learning, it also makes productive English sound more natural, and it helps students to understand that texts are not composed word by word, but chunk by chunk.

Sample text
Upper-intermediate

Constable picture wins the Turner (no, not that Constable)

THE video is, according to one art critic, mesmerising. Twenty-six uniformed policemen and women stare into the camera, silent and seemingly immobile for 60 minutes. It ends with one officer uttering a dramatic yelp of anger and relief at being allowed to move at last.

Yesterday, Gillian Wearing's offbeat work helped her win the Turner prize and a cheque for £20,000. Miss Wearing, a 34-year-old documentary maker and graduate of the Chelsea School of Art, was chosen from an all-female shortlist of four for the award designed to honour Britain's best young artists.

Entitled *Sixty Minutes of Silence*, the video's uniqueness appears to lie in the fact that for most of the hour nothing actually happens. Stern, blank faces gaze unflinchingly into the camera. With tension mounting, there is suddenly a sound, a slight movement among the posed ranks. An unseen shuffling of feet gradually grows louder, building up to the scream from the officer at the end.

(Adapted from the *Daily Mail*, 3 Dec. 1997, p. 17)

5.4 Write and remove

LEVEL

Intermediate and above

TIME

30–40 minutes

AIMS

To develop vocabulary; to practise gap-filling techniques; to help with memory training.

MATERIALS

Copies of the texts (see 'Preparation'); correction fluid; and paper for each group.

PREPARATION

Find two texts a little above the students' level that contain up to 20 new words. Newspaper and authentic sources are good, especially on business and technological topics such as telecommunications. Make enough copies so that each person either has text A or text B.

PROCEDURE

1 Give half the class two copies of one text (A), the other half two copies of the second text (B). Divide them into pairs or small groups and tell them that you want them to be the experts on their text in ten minutes. They can read it as many times as they want, checking any new words or expressions. However, every time they check something in their dictionary, they must blank it out from one of the copies they are working with, and write it on a piece of paper. It works best if the words are jumbled all over the piece of paper. One copy of the text is the master copy, and must not be altered.

2 The 'A' and 'B' groups swap the pieces of paper with the words they have checked, so that everyone is looking through vocabulary from a text they have not seen. They do not swap their original texts. Allow five minutes for looking up any words they don't know, and for discussion. Can they guess what sort of text the words came from? What might it be about?

3 Each group passes on their copy of the original text with blanked-out words and expressions to the group that has been looking at their word list.

4 They read the gapped text to confirm their guesses about what type of text it is. Then they recreate the original texts by filling the gaps with the vocabulary from the jumbled page.

5 They check their answers against the unaltered master copy.

VARIATION

At elementary level, give each group a single copy of the same text. They remove the vocabulary they check in the dictionary, but they do not write it on a piece of paper. Instead, they swap their copies as in step 3 above and fill in the gaps from memory.

5.5 Board words

LEVEL	All

TIME	30 minutes +

AIMS	**To help students make associations between words; memory training.**

MATERIALS	A copy of the text and a dictionary for each student.

PREPARATION	1 Find a text containing ten or more vocabulary items new to the class and make a copy for everyone.
	2 At the beginning of the lesson, draw an empty grid on the board with at least as many boxes as there are words you want to focus on. It is a good idea to allow 5–10 extra boxes.

PROCEDURE	1 Give out the text and ask the students to work through it in pairs to find out what it's about. They should also make a note of the vocabulary they would like to check. Do not allow them to use a dictionary yet.
	2 Ask the class what they think the text is about. Then ask what words they would like to look up, and as they call them out, write them up in the boxes of the grid on the board in random order.
	3 The students look up the words in the grid and any others they want from the text.
	4 Ask if anyone looked up any other words and add them to the grid. Then each pair must choose two words and make a possible association between them. The rest of the class judge whether the association is acceptable.

Sample text
Intermediate

WHEN it comes to aerial photography, it's best to call in an expert. So when wildlife film-maker John Downer wanted a bird's-eye view of the Italian Alps, he handed his camera over to a golden eagle.

Dipping and soaring over snow-capped peaks in the shadow of the Matterhorn, the bird, with a specially adapted video camera strapped to his back, created the ultimate in-flight movie.

The hand-reared eagle, named Kintyre, spent weeks training with his owner for his film debut. The 12-year-old bird spent many hours becoming accustomed to wearing the hand-tailored harness and camera.

The camera itself weighed only a pound, but to make the load more comfortable, some parts were strapped underneath the bird, no heavier than if he had been carrying prey in his talons. As for the location, Kintyre didn't have to worry about flying himself there. He arrived, like the rest of his back-up crew, on a plane.

Then he was released among the high peaks, his owner on hand to make sure he came back to earth. Kintyre captured more than just fantastic views from his 5ft wingspan. He managed to swivel the camera to catch other golden eagles in flight, wheeling and banking and plummeting down on prey.

(Adapted from the *Daily Mail*, 3 Dec. 1997, p. 3)

Possible board grid

call in	strapped	back-up	earth
bird's-eye view	swivel	peaks	prey
dipping	eagle	snow-capped	underneath
location	load	released	soared

Possible answers
– *bird's-eye view* and *soared* go together because when the bird was soaring high in the sky, the pictures from the camera gave a bird's-eye view;
– *snow-capped* goes with *peaks*, as the tops of mountains have got snow on them in winter;
– an *eagle* is a bird that hunts for *prey*;
– *soar*, *dip*, and *swivel* are types of movement.

Acknowledgements
This activity is based on an idea in Redman and Ellis, *A Way with Words* (see Further Reading, page 167).

5.6 'Would-be' vocabulary

LEVEL

Intermediate and above

TIME

20 minutes

AIMS

To encourage students to think about their reactions to words; to make guesses about the usefulness of new vocabulary.

MATERIALS

A copy of the text, the worksheet, and a dictionary for each student.

PREPARATION

Find a suitable text on a topic of interest with up to 15 new words or expressions for the class; semi-specialized texts on scientific discoveries, or adventures in exotic locations, or job descriptions work well. Make copies for everyone, and of the 'Would-be vocabulary' worksheet.

PROCEDURE

1 Give out the text and ask the students to find out the general topic, checking any new words in their dictionaries.
2 In pairs, the students compare their reactions to the text. Then they fill in the worksheet individually, first completing the two sentences appropriately, then putting the words and expressions from the text in the appropriate group.

WOULD-BE VOCABULARY

Put the words and expressions from the text into the appropriate group:

These words are useful for me now

These words will be useful for me when …

These words would be useful for me if …

---

3 Ask the students to compare their answers in groups of four and to discuss any differences.

5.7 Word profiles

LEVEL

Elementary and above

TIME

30 minutes

AIMS

To help students contextualize vocabulary.

MATERIALS

A copy of the grid on the next page for each student; a dictionary for each group.

PREPARATION

1 If you want to use this as a pre-reading activity: find a suitable text with 10–15 new words and make copies of the text for everyone. Texts where the writer expresses strong views are good: controversies, interviews, and reviews work well.

2 Make a copy of the grid for each student.

PROCEDURE

1 If you are presenting vocabulary, write 10–15 new pieces of vocabulary on the board, and ask the students, in groups of three, to select up to five words each. They should write them in the left-hand column of the grid. Make sure that all the words are accounted for.

2 Explain to the students that they must find out how the words are used, who uses them, in what sort of situation, and what the writer's attitude towards them is. Ask the students to complete the grid with this information in note form, using the dictionary as a source. They can leave blanks if they are not sure of any details. One example has been done from the text on page 137.

Word	Who uses it?	What are they talking about?
1 *ground-breaking*	*reviewer or expert*	*something new— here new musical style*
2		
3		
4		
5		

3 The students circulate around class explaining their words. They do not need to take notes on what they hear—some of the information might not be accurate or appropriate in the context.

4 Give out the text from which the items were taken. After they have read them through, the students check in their dictionaries to see if their ideas were correct, and if the words in the text are used as they had expected. They make any corrections necessary.

5 The students circulate again and either correct what they said in step 3, or confirm the accuracy of their guesses. This is a nice non-threatening way of 'correcting' and is very communicative.

VARIATION

To use this activity as a recap, elicit from the students 15–20 words recently encountered, and ask them to complete the grids from memory for 5–10 words. They circulate to compare notes with one another.

COMMENTS

Some students find this a handy way of committing words to memory, and adopt this grid idea as a way of noting down new vocabulary in their books.

Sample text
Advanced

REVIEWS:

Great depression

THEIR debut album, *Dummy*, won the Mercury Prize a couple of years ago, thanks to its ground-breaking fusion of hip-hop rhythms and ethereal vocals. Before long, dinner parties were being conducted to the sound of Beth Gibbon's anguished wailings and whimperings, against a backdrop of spooky beats, weird noises and what sounded like samples from outer space. Almost overnight, *Portishead* had become deeply trendy.

If there were an award for miserableness, Portishead would walk away with that, too. For all their invention and newness of music—sometimes they sound like nothing you've ever heard before—they make distinctly uneasy listening. This is especially true live (you can't turn them down or put something more cheerful on) and the London leg of their UK tour was one of the most enervating concerts I can remember.

Gibbon's voice may cover an even greater tonal range than before, but what she actually sings about is more or less the same thing, over and over: obsession, loneliness, self-loathing. Even so, it was performed here with admirable diligence, economy and restraint, with some particularly snappy drumming, and illuminated by lights and effects which matched the music to perfection.

But instrumental virtuosity and technical trickery could not disguise the awful emptiness at the heart of this show, and after an hour and a half of bleak soundscapes it came as a huge relief when a second encore failed to materialise.

(Adapted from the *Daily Telegraph*, 28 Nov. 1997, p. 25)

5.8 Writer's slant

LEVEL — **Elementary and above**

TIME — **30 minutes +**

AIMS — **To develop an awareness of the writer's position in a text; awareness of register as a means of expressing attitude.**

MATERIALS — A suitable text; a dictionary for each pair.

PREPARATION — Find a text where the writer has strong opinion about what he or she is writing about. Articles about controversial topics, travel descriptions, readers' letters and interviews with famous or successful people work well. Make enough copies for everyone (make sure you observe copyright law).

PROCEDURE —

1 Write the title or topic of the text on the board and ask the class whether they think the text will be positive or negative, and how they will know.

2 Give out the text and ask the students to read through quickly to see what the author's opinion is. How do they know? Elicit or explain that writers show their opinions in what they say, and how they say it—that includes grammar, vocabulary, register, and style.

3 The students go through the text underlining every word or expression—including those that are new to them—that could have a positive or negative meaning (without dictionaries at this stage). Ask them to check their ideas in pairs.

4 They use the dictionary to confirm their guesses, paying attention to dictionary codes that reveal attitude and emotion, for example, 'euph', 'fam', 'derog', '!'.

FOLLOW-UP

For homework the students produce an 'answer' to the writer's text, with the opposite viewpoint.

5.9 Talking walls

LEVEL

Elementary and above

TIME

30 minutes

AIMS

Idiomatic vocabulary development; memory training.

MATERIALS

Copies of the texts (see 'Preparation'); pieces of card; adhesive plaster or similar; a dictionary for each 3–4 students.

PREPARATION

1 Find a short text at a suitable level with lots of idiomatic language—stories from popular magazines, book and film reviews, pop interviews, or song lyrics work well.
2 Choose 10–20 **idioms** or expressions from the text and write each word of each idiom or expression on a large piece of card. Stick the individual cards up around the classroom.

PROCEDURE

1 Show the students the cards around the room and tell them they are words from English idioms and expressions.
2 Divide the class into groups of three or four. They all walk around the room looking at the cards, trying to work out the idioms and expressions.
3 Back at their desks, the groups check their dictionaries to confirm their guesses and to work out the meanings of the idioms or expressions. Tell them you are going to give them a text to read, and ask them to predict the general topic.
4 Give out the text. The groups read it through to see:
    – if they were right about the topic;
    – what the chosen idioms or expressions are;
    – what they mean in the context.
5 After you have read and discussed the text, divide it into as many sections as there are groups. Each group takes the idioms from their respective section off the walls as quickly as possible.
6 Go round the groups in turn, asking each to summarize their part of the text from memory, using their idioms or expressions as prompts.

VARIATION	You can use this activity to recap idioms or expressions from previous lessons.

1 Put the students in groups of three or four.

2 Each group writes out five recently learnt idioms or expressions, one word per card, then puts the cards up in one part of the room.

3 Everyone circulates and tries to spot the other groups' idioms.

4 Back in their places, the groups list all the idioms they remembered and discuss where they first came across them.

5.10 A number of meanings

LEVEL	**Lower-intermediate and above**
TIME	**30 minutes +**
AIMS	**To help students deal with words with more than one meaning.**
MATERIALS	A class set of dictionaries; copies of the text.
PREPARATION	Find a short text at a suitable level which contains a number of words with more than one meaning listed in the dictionary (or make up your own). Newspaper extracts work quite well. Underline or highlight the terms with more than one meaning (see the example below). Divide the text into two parts.

Example

A	B
A <u>former</u> waiter <u>posed</u> as a millionaire after stealing one of his employer's <u>luxury</u> cars and <u>threw</u> a <u>party</u> in the <u>house</u> in a <u>smart</u> London suburb when he knew the owner would be away. He <u>drew</u> up a <u>guest</u> list of <u>over</u> 100 <u>rich</u> and famous <u>people</u>, and sent them <u>personal</u> invitation by Rolls Royce, asking them to <u>arrive</u> at midnight for a <u>special occasion</u>. Hundreds <u>turned up</u> and had a <u>great time</u> enjoying the host's expensive wines and fine food.	THE POLICE turned up a short while later after neighbours complained about the noise. 'We were sick of the sound of people laughing and dancing', one complained. When they arrived in the drive of the three-storey house, the waiter realised that he was in trouble so, to escape from the situation, he changed his jacket and pretended to be a simple waiter again, even offering the police a drink while they looked for the 'owner' of the house.

Photocopiable © Oxford University Press

PROCEDURE	1 Give out the text and ask the students to look at part A. Explain that all the underlined words can be used in more than one sense. Ask the class to look up 'former' in their dictionaries. Which meaning is the right one here? Ask how many different meanings there are, and how they know which is best. Does their dictionary number the different meanings?

2 When the class has seen this example, ask them to look up all the underlined words and to write the number of the particular meaning next to or above the word in question.

3 The students check in pairs. Explain that sometimes the meaning they want is not the first meaning given in the **entry**—it is good training to look through all the meanings quickly.

4 Ask the pairs to think which other words in the rest of the text (part B) have more than one meaning. First they should guess, then check in their dictionaries and again write the number next to the appropriate word.

5 Take feedback, and check the answers.

5.11 Weather words and global warming

LEVEL	**Intermediate and above**
TIME	**30–45 minutes**
AIMS	**Vocabulary development: weather words.**
MATERIALS	A newspaper weather forecast or report with world temperatures (in English if possible, although with monolingual classes you can use pages from a first-language newspaper); maps, charts, and encyclopedias; a dictionary for each group of three.
PREPARATION	Make a copy of the forecast for each group of three or four students.
PROCEDURE	1 Put the students in groups of three or four and ask them to think of a city somewhere in the world for every letter of the alphabet. They can make use of the maps, charts, and encyclopedias if required. They should cover as many different countries and continents as possible and list the cities on a piece of paper. Make sure each group has at least 20 places listed—give prompts from the weather report if necessary.

2 Explain that you want them to think of a weather word—a noun, verb, or adjective—to go with each place name. The word must begin with the same letter of the alphabet for each place; however, the weather word doesn't have to be the perfect description of the place—in fact, the more unusual the better (so that Algiers could be 'Arctic', and Fez 'freezing'). Try to avoid the obvious words like *hot*, *rainy*, or *cold*, and explain that each group should try to find words they don't think the other groups will have thought of. The groups leaf through their dictionaries to find weather if where they cannot think of any.

3 Give a copy of the weather report to each group and ask them to see how many of the same cities they had; then they see how

similar or different the weather word they suggested was compared to the actual weather given in the report.

4 The groups write a weather report for today for one area of the world, based on their own words and cities, and compare and contrast this with the newspaper report, explaining how global warming has been responsible for the changes.

5 Stick the reports up around the class, and invite everyone to circulate and see how their own part of the world was affected, and where the most dramatic changes occurred. Which is the most unlikely? Which the most fun?

COMMENTS

Some students may worry that they haven't got the same cities as in the report. They can substitute their geographically nearest guess (for example, Adelaide, Wellington, or Manila could do for Sydney).

5.12 Self-correction

LEVEL

All

TIME

10 minutes

AIMS

To encourage students to use dictionaries to check and correct their writing.

MATERIALS

Dictionaries.

PROCEDURE

1 Before you set a writing task, discuss with the students how they prepare to write and what their strategies are. How many of them use a dictionary? What do they check? Do they use a dictionary before, during, or after writing, or all three? You will probably find that dictionaries are rarely consulted in the post-writing editorial stage.

2 Explain that you want them to check five words or phrases in the dictionary *after* they have written, but before they hand in their work. It can be anything they want—spelling, grammar, meaning—but they must check and underline five things. If possible, make time available in class for everyone to do this at the same time. Go round the class and if you see problems, point out where they could profitably use the dictionary.

3 Take in the work and correct it as normal. If there are no mistakes with the underlined parts, tick them or mark them with your positive symbol to encourage the habit of checking with the dictionary.

5.13 Writing

LEVEL

Elementary and above

TIME

Lesson 1: 10–20 minutes
Lesson 2: 10 minutes

AIMS

To encourage students to use a dictionary in the planning stage of a writing task; to develop an awareness of common word partnerships and *collocations*.

MATERIALS

A dictionary for each pair of students.

PREPARATION

Prepare the class for a writing task as normal.

PROCEDURE

1 Before your class begins a writing task, write up the theme on the board or overhead projector and ask the students in pairs to brainstorm 15–30 key words they associate with the theme and which they might use in the composition.

2 Put the pairs together in fours, and ask them to compare their notes. Give each pair a dictionary and ask them to look up at least ten of the key words they had suggested. Ask them to look in particular for word combinations, adjectives that go with nouns, prepositions or adverbs that go with verbs, and so on, and to make a note of any they think they could use. Explain that such combinations often add interesting details and make texts sound more natural.

3 The groups discuss how they could use the information they have found, and prepare an outline for their composition. Then, either in the lesson or for homework, they write their compositions using as many of the details found in step 2 as possible.

4 Correct the essays as normal, but also make a list of all the combinations you think the students found in the dictionaries, and in the next lesson write them on the board or overhead projector. Ask the class to read through the combinations quietly, seeing if they can spot their own, and imagining the meaning of the others.

5 Divide the class into groups of six to eight and ask them to go through the list, explaining which partnerships they used. If there are any unclaimed partnerships, everyone checks in the dictionary.

6 Discuss the answers.

5.14 Dictionary dictation

LEVEL	**Elementary and above**
TIME	**20 minutes +**
AIMS	**To encourage use of the dictionary to check written work.**
MATERIALS	A text for dictation; a dictionary for each student.
PREPARATION	Find a suitable text for a dictation.
PROCEDURE	1 Prepare your class for a dictation in the normal way. Before you read, put the title or the topic on the board or overhead transparency and ask the students to work in pairs and to imagine what they think the dictation will be about. Ask them to call out words or ideas they think will be in the text. Give feedback about their guesses, telling them whether or not they are right.

2 Allow five minutes for the students to check in the dictionary before you read—they can look for key words, and from there check possible **collocations**, grammar information, spelling, and so on.

3 Read the dictation normally.

4 Give the class five minutes to check anything they want in the dictionary before you go through the answers or take the work in.

Acknowledgements
This is a version of an activity suggested by Adrian Underhill in *Dictionaries, Lexicography and Language Learning* (ed. Ilson, 1985).

5.15 Compound texts

LEVEL	**Elementary and above**
TIME	**25 minutes +**
AIMS	**To raise awareness of the frequency of *compounds* in English; vocabulary development.**
MATERIALS	Copies of the text (see 'Preparation'); a dictionary for each pair.
PREPARATION	1 Find or invent a text containing 5–15 compound words: newspaper stories with a factual or technical slant and (for advanced students) poems are possible sources. Make a copy for each student.

2 Write one word of each compound on one piece of paper (A), the other on a second piece (B), and make enough copies so everyone has either A or B.

PROCEDURE

1 Put the class in pairs and give each pair either the A or B list of words. Explain that each list contains one part of a compound word.

2 The pairs discuss:
   – whether their words are the first or last part of the compounds
   – how to complete their compounds.

   They can refer to the dictionary for help.

3 Put A and B pairs together in fours, and ask them to see if they can match the two halves to form all the compounds, using dictionaries for confirmation.

4 Tell them that all of these words come from a text they are going to read. They discuss what they think the text will be about.

5 Distribute the text and ask the students to confirm their guesses.

Sample text

A CRAZED passenger attacked a British pilot as he landed a jumbo jet with 300 people on board. The man, who was clutching a whisky bottle, forced his way into the cockpit and tried to pull the captain out of his seat. The pilot fought him off then radioed for police at the airport while crew members and three business class passengers restrained the burly attacker as the jet neared Bangkok.

Last night, the pilot, who has not been named, was hailed a hero by passenger Charles Adams, who broke his hand when he punched the manic passenger.

'I have nothing but praise for the two British guys—the pilot and co-pilot—at the controls,' said Mr Adams. 'They kept their heads. I think the passenger had a drug problem or something like that. He ran towards the cockpit and went through the open door leading to the flight deck. I decided I'd better assist—the last thing the crew wanted was a madman in there as they were trying to land the plane. We eventually dragged the man to the ground, and someone put handcuffs on him.'

(Adapted from the *Daily Mail*, 4 Dec. 1997, p. 7)

A				B			
hand	flight	co-	drug	bottle	port	pilot	jet
jumbo	whisky	air		class	cuffs	deck	
business	mad	crew		problem	members		
				man			

5.16 Coded prepositions

LEVEL   **Elementary and above**

TIME   **30 minutes**

AIMS   **Working with dependent prepositions.**

MATERIALS   Copies of the text and worksheet; a dictionary for each pair.

PREPARATION   1 Find a text with 10–15 verb-and-dependent preposition
                        structures or with prepositional phrases: newspaper reports
                        work well, since they often focus on times, dates, places and
                        dramatic actions done by people in specific situations. Make a
                        copy for each pair of students.
                     2 Make a copy of the 'What's missing?' worksheet for each
                        student, or create one at a suitable level.

PROCEDURE   1 Give the students a copy of the worksheet and ask them to find
                        out as quickly as possible what is missing.
                     2 In pairs, the students go through the worksheet, guessing which
                        prepositions the symbols have replaced. (There is an answer
                        key on page 149.)

WHAT'S MISSING?

Elementary

Read through this text to find the missing prepositions. Each
symbol represents one preposition.

It was Rob's birthday, and I had a lot to do before I would be
ready # the party @ nine that evening. I was looking forward ~
the party. I had already decided + the clothes I wanted to wear
(and had paid a lot * money + a new pair of shoes to go ∧ the
jacket I had bought). But what could I buy # Rob? I knew he was
keen + reading, and that he was really good @ most sports, too,
but that didn't really help me ∧ my problem. I didn't want to
waste my money + something that he already had, so I decided
to talk ~ his mother to see if she could give me any ideas.

So I rang her and asked her # some help. Once I had
explained my problem ~ her, I asked if she could think * a
suitable present # him.

'It's very kind * you,' she said. 'But of course it all depends +
how much you can afford.'

I was a bit short * money then, actually, so I had to be careful.

Anyway, she was full * ideas. % fact I was so busy shopping
that I was nearly late # the party.

Code: 1. # __   2. @ __   3. ~ __   4. + __   5. * __   6. ∧ __   7. % __

Photocopiable © Oxford University Press

3 They confirm their ideas in the dictionary. Check their answers against the key at the end of the chapter.

4 Give a copy of the text to each pair and ask them to use their own system of symbols to adapt it as in the worksheet.

5 The pairs swap their versions of the adapted text and try to recreate the original.

VARIATION 1

The students work on different parts of the same text, or on different texts altogether, and then swap texts around the class.

VARIATION 2

All the students work on the same text. Take in their texts when they have substituted their symbols for the prepositions. Return the student versions in the next lesson and see if they can recall the missing prepositions.

COMMENTS

This activity introduces an enjoyable problem-solving aspect to an area of language that worries many students. They often respond very positively.

Acknowledgements
I first learnt this technique from Seth Lindstromberg.

5.17 Fill that gap

LEVEL

Intermediate and above

TIME

30–45 minutes

AIMS

To practise multiple-choice gap-fill skills; to encourage discussion; to help with memory development.

MATERIALS

Correction fluid and suitable texts; a dictionary for each pair or group.

PREPARATION

Select two or four texts in English 10–20 lines long, at an appropriate level. They could be taken from the coursebook and used for revision purposes; otherwise texts with a strong storyline, crime reports, or stories of accidents are good sources.

PROCEDURE

1 Put the class in pairs or small groups and give each group two copies of the same text. Allow them five minutes to find out what the text is about and to check any words they want.

2 Each group uses one copy of their text to create a gap-fill to test the other groups. One copy will be the master for correction purposes; the other is the one they can work on. They choose 10–20 words from the original and check them in the dictionary. They delete the original words from one copy, and number the gaps.

3 The groups choose three other words from the same page in the dictionary as the deleted words, and write the four options beside or at the bottom of the text on the second copy to create the multiple-choice answers. They must be sure that only one of the options actually fits.

4 The groups swap their gap-fill texts with the multiple-choice options, and complete them without using dictionaries.

5 The groups check their answers in their dictionaries. When they feel confident of their answers, they check with the master copies.

VARIATION

At step 3, you can take in and photocopy all the texts so that each student can go home with one to complete for homework. Then, next lesson, the students who worked on the same text check their answers together.

Sample text

THE waiting 'quad' bikes looked squat and powerful, each with four fat wheels spread wide below a broad, comfortable seat and wide, strong handlebars. I slid my leg over the nearest and settled into a comfortable wide seat, legs cocooned by the broad sweeps of the bodywork that covered the wide tyres.

As a motorcyclist, I found the controls familiar: the handlebars had levers for the clutch and front brake, while the rear brake and gear-change were down by the serrated foot-rests. I tried to twist the throttle and found the first difference: there was a lever, too.

The others in our group had ridden 'quads' before but I had not. Our guide for the day, Dave, handed out gloves, crash helmets and goggles and ran quickly through some instructions. First, a safety tip: 'The foot-rests are for your feet, even when stationary. Trailing feet can get caught under the back wheels.'

'The desert is very fragile. You can still see the tracks left by the ox-carts of the first pioneers. So, when we leave the practice area, you don't just follow me—you stick right in my tracks.'

(Adapted from the *Financial Times Weekend*, 22/23 Nov. 1997, p. XIII)

5.18 Collecting collocations

LEVEL

Intermediate and above

TIME

20–30 minutes

AIMS

To practise reading skills; to raise awareness of *collocations*.

MATERIALS

Suitable text (see the example on page 149); dictionary for each pair; white-out or black pen to blank out words from the text for each pair.

PREPARATION

Find a text at a suitable level: authentic sources such as newspapers and magazines are good, as are literary and popular fiction. Topics can reflect the theme of the coursebook—crime, jobs, relationships. Texts should be between 200 and 500 words.

PROCEDURE

1 Divide the class into pairs and give out the text. They read the texts so that they can summarize the main points clearly.

2 Explain that you want the pairs to find common word partnerships—collocations—in their text. Elicit examples from the text: *experience anxiety, job interview, bound to be, active lifestyle, stresses and strains,* and *take a bus* are collocations from the first paragraph of the example below. It doesn't matter if pairs find different collocations, but both members of each pair must agree on the collocations they find.

3 Explain that there are 'strong' and 'weak' collocations. Strong collocations are relatively fixed and frequently co-occur, like 'fish and *chips*', 'strong *coffee*'; weak collocations are less common partnerships like 'experience anxiety' in the first paragraph of the sample text. How many of their collocations are 'strong' enough to feature in their dictionary? Allow five minutes for them to check.

4 One half of the class delete the first word of the collocations they have found, and the other half delete the second. They do this for 10–20 examples.

5 Pairs who deleted the first word of each collocation exchange their texts (with deletions) with pairs who deleted the second words.

6 The students complete the collocations from memory or by referring to a dictionary.

7 The pairs work in fours to check their answers. How many collocations did they remember correctly?

Sample text

E veryone experiences anxiety, depression and tension at times. For students examinations and job interviews are examples of situations that are bound to be stressful. Those who always have an active lifestyle are best able to cope with the stresses and strains of their lives.

It is a mistake to abandon walking and take a bus to save ten minutes when an exam looms, or to relax in a bar rather than playing sports after a day at college. The best advice is to make exercise part of your daily life: research has shown that this is better than relying on a drink or a smoke to relax you.

- Use stairs rather than lifts
- Walk or cycle rather than going by car or bus
- Try different games and sports: play the ones that you enjoy
- Exercise for fifteen minutes three days each week

People take exercise for many reasons

The best reason is for fun. Most of us enjoy taking part in sport, and improving our performance. We feel better if we are moderately active, and do not spend all our spare time sitting around indoors.

The physical benefits of exercising depend on the type and amount. Exercises like weight lifting increase muscular strength, running helps the heart and circulation to function at their best, and others, like yoga and keep-fit, improve flexibility.

Some benefits of habitual exercise may only become apparent as time passes. Active people recover more quickly from illness and operations, get less back pain and are less likely than the inactive to suffer from broken bones as a result of osteoporosis (bone thinning).

There are also psychological advantages to being physically active. At all ages and stages of life, an active lifestyle helps clear thinking and makes it easier to cope with stressful situations and depression.

(From *Less Stress, More Success: a Student Guide.* The Health Promotion Trust)

Answers

5.16 **1** for; **2** at; **3** to; **4** on; **5** of; **6** with; **7** in.

6 Using bilingual dictionaries

Translation is a natural element of language learning, but it is full of pitfalls for the unwary. Both translation and the bilingual dictionaries that students generally use for this purpose have been out of favour in the EFL classroom for a long time. There are, however, signs that this is changing.

The first activities in this section help raise students' awareness of some of the weaknesses of bilingual dictionaries in terms of the quantity, quality, and presentation of information they include (6.1, 'One more improvement', page 151; 6.2, 'Cross-checking bilingual dictionaries', page 152) and look at students' learning preferences (6.3, 'Text comprehension', page 153) when dealing with texts.

The focus changes with 6.6, 'Sounds the same?' (page 156) and 6.7, 'Bilingual idioms' (page 158), which look at how the sound system of English is exploited in alliterative and idiomatic expressions, and invite students to make comparisons with their own language.

6.5, 'Project words' (page 155) and 6.8, 'Pelman translation' (page 159) encourage students to use bilingual dictionaries to generate and remember vocabulary, and 6.9, 'Doctors' bilingual dictionaries' (page 160) compares how **collocation** is treated in bilingual and monolingual dictionaries.

For the activities in this chapter, any bilingual dictionary can be used, even pocket versions and electronic dictionaries with translating functions, since the insights will be similar. However, larger dictionaries are generally more productive.

6.1 One more improvement

LEVEL Elementary and above

TIME 35 minutes +

AIMS To encourage students to think critically about their dictionaries.

MATERIALS Enough bilingual and monolingual dictionaries for each pair to have one of each; a copy of the 'Dictionary quiz' worksheet for each student (or make a similar one).

PROCEDURE 1 Put the students in pairs and give each pair either a monolingual or a bilingual dictionary. Give each pair a copy of the worksheet. (There is an answer key at the end of the chapter, page 161.)

DICTIONARY QUIZ
Intermediate

Use your dictionary to find the answers to these questions:

1 Do you **pick** or **pull** a fight with someone?

2 Do you **make** or **do** an excuse?

3 Which word does not form a compound with **eye**: lid/patch/friend/shadow/opener?

4 Where will you find a **busker**?

5 How do you feel if you are **hassled**?

6 Which is the odd one out: **crunch/munch/sip/nibble**?

7 Do we say:

   a We had lovely weather last week? *or*

   b We had a lovely weather last week?

8 Which is bigger, a **rabbit** or a **hare**?

9 Do we say **sea bank** or **seashore**?

10 Which word has the same stress as **redundant**: important/document/government?

Photocopiable © Oxford University Press

2 Ask the pairs to work together in fours, comparing the answers from different dictionaries. What information was missing from which type of dictionary?

3 Tell the students that some publishers have invited suggestions about how their dictionaries can be improved. Ask the groups of four to look through their dictionaries and discuss what

improvements they would suggest. If necessary, give prompts, for example:

– include pictures;
– more examples;
– larger type;
– some more translations.

4 How many suggestions did the groups think of? Can they put them into an order of priority?

5 In the light of their suggested improvements, what advice would they give people using the different dictionaries? For example:

– always check that you have the right meaning of a word;
– check the pronunciation with a friend.

6.2 Cross-checking bilingual dictionaries

LEVEL   **Intermediate and above**

TIME   **10 minutes**

AIMS   **To raise awareness of the gaps in bilingual dictionaries.**

MATERIALS   Copies of the text, bilingual dictionaries for every four students.

PREPARATION   1 Choose a text dealing with a dramatic or unusual event. Poems and song lyrics where language is used to special effect also work well.

2 Prepare a list of 10–15 key vocabulary items, if possible including **collocations**, unusual intensifiers, and idiomatic turns of phrase (for example, *splitting headache, fall flat on your face, dead on time*). These could be new words, **false friends,** or words which have several different meanings. Make copies of the text and the word list for everyone.

PROCEDURE   1 Tell the class the title of the text you are about to study. Elicit what they think it will be about. Give out the list of 10–15 vocabulary items from the text and ask the class how many of the words they already know.

2 The students check the meaning of the words in both sections of their dictionary: first they should check the English section to see what definitions, collocations, explanations and translations are given. Then they should look up the same words in their language and see if all the same information is given there too. Ask them to imagine how the words will be used in the text.

3 In groups of four, the students compare what they have found. Take class feedback: what differences have they noticed? Generally they notice that there is a big difference between decoding and encoding: that is, the expressions may feature in English, but not in the mother tongue (in dictionaries produced in English-speaking countries) so that students could never produce the typical English expression by using their dictionary—or the other way round with dictionaries produced in non-English-speaking countries.

4 Give out the reading text and ask the groups to confirm their guesses from step 2. Do the uses of the words in the text correspond to the meanings they found in the English or mother-tongue sections of their dictionaries?

5 In their groups, the students brainstorm how to avoid such problems and see what they come up with. Typical answers include:
   – using a bilingual dictionary and cross-checking in a monolingual dictionary;
   – thinking of the key word in the mother tongue, then cross-checking the English entries for the key words for collocations or other typical expressions;
   – only using a monolingual dictionary;
   – getting into the habit of noting and learning English words in contexts and collocations.

6.3 Text comprehension

LEVEL	**All**
TIME	**30 minutes +**
AIMS	**To compare how bilingual dictionaries and learners' dictionaries help with reading comprehension; memory training.**
MATERIALS	Bilingual dictionaries for half the class; monolingual dictionaries for the others; copies of the text in English.
PREPARATION	Find a suitable text of 300 or more words which includes ten or more new words or expressions. With more advanced classes, texts with idiomatic expressions and several **homonyms** are good. Make copies for everyone.
PROCEDURE	1 Put the class in pairs, and give half the class bilingual dictionaries, the other half monolingual dictionaries. Give out the text and ask the class to read it through to see what it is about.

2 The students can look up as many words as they want. Tell them to look for as much information about the words they check as possible, for example:

– what grammar patterns do they occur in?
– how do you pronounce them?
– do they have other meanings?
– are there occasions when they are not appropriate?

3 The pairs who worked with the same dictionaries discuss which words they have looked up, what they mean in that particular context and anything else they noticed.

4 Now combine pairs who used bilingual and monolingual dictionaries. They discuss their understanding of the text and the vocabulary. Did they look up the same words? If so, do they agree on the meaning?

5 Write all the words the class checked in their respective dictionaries on the board. Go through the list asking what the words mean and how they are used.

6 Ask the class if both types of dictionary provide the same information.

FOLLOW-UP   Next lesson, the pairs swap roles and work with the other dictionary on a new text. At the end of the reading comprehension, have a discussion about which dictionary they preferred using, which gave most information, which helped them understand the text more accurately, and which helped them remember the words better.

6.4 Headlines

LEVEL   **Upper-intermediate and above**

TIME   **30 minutes +**

AIMS   **To introduce students to newspaper headline language; to compare monolingual and bilingual dictionaries' treatment of this specialized language; to give an insight into the information missing from bilingual dictionaries.**

MATERIALS   Newspaper headlines and articles; bilingual and monolingual dictionaries for each pair.

PREPARATION   Collect 5–10 recent newspaper articles in English, with their headlines.

PROCEDURE

1 Write the headlines on the board. Put the students in pairs, some with bilingual dictionaries, others with monolingual dictionaries, and ask them to guess what the stories might be about, using their dictionaries to check any new words. Encourage discussion.

2 Ask pairs who used the different types of dictionary to work together and compare notes.

3 Put up the original texts around the room and ask everyone to check to see what they were actually about.

4 Ask the students if the dictionaries gave the right sort of information. How helpful were the bilingual ones? Why is there less information in them?

COMMENTS

This activity works well with many language items: phrasal verbs, delexical verbs like *have*, *take*, *go*, and with words with more than one meaning—and can be used with sentence-level translation and reading comprehension.

6.5 Project words

LEVEL

Intermediate and above

TIME

40–60 minutes

AIMS

Vocabulary development

MATERIALS

Enough mono- and bilingual dictionaries for each student to have one or the other; copies of the text.

PREPARATION

Find a text on a theme you are working on that you think the class will be interested in, and make a copy for each student.

PROCEDURE

1 Write the theme on the board or overhead transparency and ask the class for a couple of examples of vocabulary they associate with it.

2 Divide the class into an even number of small groups. Half the groups work in their own language (or languages: see 'Variation') and think of as many words as possible on the given theme. The other half works in English and does the same.

3 After five minutes, form new groups combining members of both groups, and ask them to see what similarities and differences they have. At this stage, they can use mono- or bilingual dictionaries to check their vocabulary lists and to explain words to their new partners.

4 Allow three to four minutes for the groups to expand their word sets a little more. They can do this by thinking of words in their mother tongue and translating, or by working in English; the important thing is that the whole group must understand all the words they come up with—this creates a lot of peer **teaching** as students explain the words they are familiar with but which others may not know.

5 As a prompt, ask them if they have thought of verbs, adjectives, and adverbs that could be used to talk about the theme—word lists tend to be dominated by nouns, and a good balance is wise! Encourage the groups to aim for a total of 50–100 words. It sounds ambitious, but students enjoy rising to the challenge.

6 Give out the text. The students read it to see how many of their words or expressions feature.

FOLLOW-UP

Students continue the text, or write a review of it, using all the words on their vocabulary lists. This can be done as homework.

VARIATION

With multilingual groups, either ask students with the same mother tongue to work together in groups in step 2, or amalgamate steps 1 and 2 and ask everyone individually to produce their word list in their first language, and then make groups that combine speakers with different mother tongues for step 3.

6.6   Sounds the same?

LEVEL

Intermediate and above (in monolingual classes)

TIME

20–30 minutes

AIMS

To practise *synonyms*; to raise awareness of the treatment of idiomatic expressions in bilingual dictionaries; to sensitize students to *alliteration* as a component of English *idioms*.

MATERIALS

A selection of mono- and bilingual dictionaries.

PREPARATION

Write a selection of alliterative sentences at a suitable level for your class.

PROCEDURE

1 Divide the class into groups of two to four, and give each group two or three alliterative idiomatic sentences in English.

   Suggested examples
   a i I bet that took a lot of time and trouble.
     ii Hold your horses.
   b i We wish him well.
     ii She's only scratched the surface.

c i He's keeping his cards close to his chest.

  ii I hope you all have happy holidays.

d i They danced till dawn.

  ii My mother made a marvellous meal.

2 The groups discuss what the sentences might mean, then translate them as naturally as possible into their own language using their bilingual dictionaries, even if this means slightly changing the drift of the sentences. Ask them if the translated sentences are longer or shorter than the English, and why? Are there any other general differences they have noticed—word order, for example? Have a quick discussion, without going too far into the original sentences.

3 The groups swap translations—but not the original English versions. Write up on the board the key alliterative letters (in the examples above: T, H, W, S, K/C, H, D, and M). They use their bilingual dictionaries to work out which is the key letter of the original sentence for the translations they now have, and to try to find the idiomatic expression and what it means. Allow a two-minute discussion.

4 Once each group has found the key letter, give them five minutes to try to recreate the original sentence with as many alliterations as possible, using their bilingual dictionaries for help.

5 The groups pass their translations to be checked by the groups with the originals. The groups must provide as much helpful feedback as possible to ensure that the translators can arrive at an accurate translation the second time around.

6 Put up the results on a display board and invite the class to circulate and compare the originals and the translations. Were any of the idioms given in the bilingual dictionaries? If so, in which section, English or the other language, or both?

COMMENTS

This is an activity for monolingual classes. It helps if you share the students' language.

VARIATION

This technique can, of course, also be used with sounds rather than initial letters, for example, diphthongs or long vowels. You can also use the technique to review vocabulary recently covered in class.

6.7 Bilingual idioms

LEVEL

Upper-intermediate and above

TIME

20–30 minutes

AIMS

To encourage discussion; to provide insights into the transparency of certain *idioms*; to raise awareness of the difficulty of word for word translation; to see how idioms are presented in bilingual dictionaries.

MATERIALS

A bilingual dictionary for each four students; copies of idioms.

PREPARATION

Make a copy of the idioms sheet for each group of three to four, or prepare your own. If you have an overhead projector, prepare a transparency of all the idioms for the final check at step 5.

PROCEDURE

1 Divide the class into groups of three to four, and give each group one of the idiom sheets A, B C, or D.

   Examples

A 1 After the match I was *black and blue*.
  2 Come here, Jon. I've *got a bone to pick with you*.
  3 I got that piece of news *from the horse's mouth*.

B 1 They've been *living from hand to mouth* since he lost his job.
  2 She wasn't being serious, she said it *tongue in cheek*.
  3 Sarah and Sam *get on like a house on fire*.

C 1 He never disagrees with the boss. He *knows which side his bread is buttered*.
  2 If you want to pass your exam you'd better *pull your socks up*.
  3 She should be careful if she starts playing squash: she's *no spring chicken*.

D 1 You really *put your foot in it* when you told her about the party.
  2 No, thanks, discos are *not my cup of tea*.
  3 He knows London *like the back of his hand*.

Photocopiable © Oxford University Press

2 Set a time limit of ten minutes. In their groups, the students discuss the possible meaning of the idioms and when it would be appropriate to use them, then propose a translation into their own language—no dictionaries yet.

3 The students check in their bilingual dictionaries. Are the idioms listed? Under which word? They write out the

translations in their own language. They translate any idioms not found in the dictionary literally.

4 The groups swap translations and discuss the meaning of the idioms, especially those translated literally, making a note of their suggestions. They do not use dictionaries for this stage.

5 Allow five minutes for the groups to find the original English idioms in their bilingual dictionaries. This is not as easy as it sounds. As they find the idioms, they should check the meanings against the suggestions they made. Were they right?

6 Put the original idioms on the board or overhead projector so that everyone can see them. Go through the meanings as a class. Ask how close the translations were and what the difficulties of translating idioms are.

COMMENTS

In multilingual groups, this activity will work as long as the nationalities are split among the groups quite evenly. A translation should be provided in each mother tongue—this can create quite a stimulating poster. Write all the different translations of an idiom on a display board; and ask students about their reactions to the different languages.

6.8 Pelman translation

LEVEL

Beginner and elementary in monolingual classes

TIME

45 minutes

AIMS

Memory work; vocabulary building.

MATERIALS

40 pieces of card for each four students; a bilingual dictionary for everyone.

PREPARATION

Find a text of 100–250 words, perhaps from a class reader or the coursebook, with up to 20 words you would like the students to focus on and learn. Cut up enough pieces of card about the same size for each word and its translation to be on a different piece.

PROCEDURE

1 Put the students in groups of four. Give out the pieces of card at the same time as you give the class the text. Ask them to read through quickly, and to check to see if they all agree the gist of the text.

2 The groups write each word they don't know or would like to check on a piece of card, and discuss what they think the translation is in their language. Ten to twenty words is a good total.

3 The students check their translations in the bilingual dictionaries, and when they agree, they write each translation

on a different piece of card. Check that the translations are accurate.

4 Divide the groups into pairs, and give one pair the cards with the translations, the other the English words. They try to recall the partner words. Allow up to five minutes for this.

5 Put the pairs in fours again. Each pair shuffles the pieces of card and puts them on the table face down. The first player turns over one card, and tries to turn over the matching translation. If he or she finds a match which everybody agrees with, he or she keeps the cards and has another go. If not, both cards must be put back where they were, face down.

6 Players take turns to try to find a matching pair until the stock of cards is exhausted.

VARIATION

When one game has been completed, the groups swap places and play again with another set.

FOLLOW-UP

The class creates cards in this manner throughout a week or so. Then you round off the final lesson with a huge game.

COMMENTS

This is an enjoyable way of providing a considerable amount of reinforcement of vocabulary, and is very popular as an end-of-class filler. The activity can also be used to recycle vocabulary recently dealt with in class.

6.9 Doctors' bilingual dictionaries

LEVEL

Elementary and above

TIME

20–30 minutes

AIMS

Vocabulary building on health problems; to check whether dictionaries have common *collocations*.

MATERIALS

Bilingual dictionaries; a copy the 'Health problems' worksheet for each pair.

PROCEDURE

1 Ask the class if there's anything they always take with them on foreign holidays. Did anyone mention a dictionary? Why or why not? Then put the class in pairs and ask them to think of the sort of health problems that you can have on holiday. In a monolingual class, they can do this in their mother tongue. If you have a multilingual class, either put pairs who speak the same language together, or ask everyone to write a list in their own language. No dictionaries at this stage.

2 Put the students in groups of six to eight and ask them to compare what they thought of, and to see how many health problems they know how to translate into English. With

multilingual groups this stage necessitates a lot of translation anyway as they compare their answers. They can check their dictionaries now.

3 Take feedback: did they have the same ideas, and did their dictionaries list all the problems they thought of? If any were missing, are they serious problems, common problems, or not?

4 Give out the worksheets and ask the students to go through it in pairs. (There is an answer key below.)

5 How many of these health problems were listed in their bilingual dictionaries? Which word were they listed under?

FOLLOW-UP

In pairs, the students prepare to mime a role-play situation with one person as a doctor, and the other as a holiday-maker with one or more of the problems on the worksheet. The rest of the class must guess what the problem is, and how it happened.

HEALTH PROBLEMS

Combine words from A with their partners from B to form some common health problems. How many can you match without using a dictionary?

A	B
1 splitting	a poisoning
2 upset	b bite
3 twisted	c headache
4 broken	d bone
5 sun	e stomach
6 food	f feet
7 pulled	g ankle
8 high	h burn
9 blistered	i muscle
10 insect	j temperature

How many of these problems are listed in your bilingual dictionary?

How many are given in your monolingual dictionary?

Are the problems given in your language? Under which word?

Photocopiable © Oxford University Press

Answers

6.1 1 pick; **2** make; **3** friend; **4** in a public place; **5** annoyed; **6** sip; **7** a; **8** hare; **9** seashore; **10** important

6.9 1 c; **2** e; **3** g; **4** d; **5** h; **6** a; **7** i; **8** j; **9** f; **10** b

Glossary of key terms

abbreviation: short form of a word, phrase, or saying, often used in dictionaries to save space; *abbr* is the abbreviation of 'abbreviation'. In many dictionaries *adj* is the abbreviation used for 'adjective'.

affix: letter or group of letters added to the beginning or end of a word to change its meaning. (See **prefix** and **suffix**.)

alliteration: when the same letter or sound occurs at the beginning of two or more words in succession. *She sells sea-shells. Come quickly.*

alphabet: set of letters or symbols in a fixed order, used when writing a language. The English alphabet has 26 letters and uses Roman script.

antonym: a word that is opposite in meaning to another, for example, *heavy–light, hot–cold.*

boundaries: divisions between linguistic units. There are boundaries between different words, and between parts of a word, for example the **stem** and the **affix**.

chunks: groups of words that occur together in a fixed or semi-fixed manner and which constitute units of meaning: *in my opinion, in a manner of speaking, see you soon.*

code: system of words, letters, and symbols used in dictionaries to present information about words and phrases in short form. Dictionaries often use codes to give information about the grammatical patterns of verbs: transitive/intransitive, taking a gerund/infinitive, and so on. This varies from dictionary to dictionary.

collocation: when words regularly occur together in a sort of partnership: *fish and chips, heavy rain, keen on, pass an exam.*

compound noun/compound word: a combination of two or more words that function together as one word. They can be one or two words, or joined by a hyphen: *policeman, flower shop, part-time.*

countable noun: a noun which has both singular and plural forms, for example, *book/books, day/days* but not *money*. Also know as **count nouns**.

defining vocabulary: a basic list of words used to explain other words. Most learner's dictionaries now use a restricted defining vocabulary.

derivative: a word formed by adding an **affix** to another word. *Unhappiness* is a derived from the adjective *happy* by adding the negative **prefix** *un-* and the noun **suffix** *-ness.*

entry: the complete set of information given about a word in a dictionary. Often dictionaries have separate entries for **homographs**. See also **headword**.

false friends: words which look similar in different languages, but which have different meanings, for example, *actual/aktuell* in German, *embarrassed/embarazada* in Spanish.

headword: a word forming a heading for a dictionary **entry**: the first word, normally in dark type.

homographs: words spelt the same way, but which have a different meaning or pronunciation: *to row a boat* and *to have a big row about something*.

homonyms: words spelt and pronounced the same way, but which have different meanings: *to book a holiday*: *to read a book*.

homophones: words which are pronounced the same but with a different spelling or meaning: *new/knew, moor/more, sea/see*.

idiom: an expression of several words which functions as a single unit, and whose meaning is different from the meaning of the individual words, for example, *see red* = get angry, *pay through the nose* = pay a lot for something.

IPA: the International Phonetic Alphabet, the system of **phonemic symbols** which can be used to describe the sounds of any language.

lexical set/lexical field/semantic field/word field: the organization of related words and expressions into a system. Parts of the body such as *neck, head, legs, fingers* form a lexical set. Other examples are words in the categories of 'food', 'colours', and 'professions'.

onomatopoeia: the imitation of natural sounds in a word to suggest what the word refers to. *Hiss, splash*, and *bang* are onomatopoeic words for the sound of a snake, of falling into water, and of a loud noise.

parts of speech: the classes that words are divided into in grammar, for example, noun, verb, adjective, conjunction, adverb, pronoun.

peer teaching: classroom teaching where one student teaches another, or a group of students.

phonemic symbols: special symbols which express the sounds of spoken words. /ə/, /ŋ/, and /θ/ are phonemic symbols for common English sounds. See also **IPA**.

phonemic transcription: the representation of a whole spoken word in a dictionary, for example as found in learner's dictionaries after the **headword** to help students pronounce the word correctly.

prefix: word or **syllable** added to the front of another word to change the meaning of that word. The prefix *un-* generally makes a word negative, for example, *happy/unhappy*.

running heads: the **headwords** from the first and last **entries** on a page, usually printed at the top of the page for guidance.

stem: the main part of a noun or verb from which other parts or words are made by adding an affix. *Work* is the stem to which you add *-s* to form *works*.

stress: the extra force used in saying some words or a **syllable** in a word. In dictionaries the stressed syllable of a word is often shown by a small raised line immediately in front of it, for example, *defeat* = /dɪˈfiːt/

suffix: a letter or group of letters added to the end of a word to form another word, for example, *late* and the suffix *-ly* form *lately*.

superordinate: a term which describes a general category of words: *vehicle* is a superordinate for a category which includes *car*, *van*, and *lorry*.

syllable: the units which a word is divided into, usually consisting of a vowel sound with a consonant sound before or after it. *Japanese* is a word of three syllables.

synonyms: different words or phrases in the same language which have the same or nearly the same meaning. *Break* and *fracture* are often synonyms: you can break or fracture your leg, but you can't fracture a promise.

usage notes: grammatical information often presented in special boxes in dictionaries, to provide details of how words are used. Often these compare and contrast related words.

word association: associating words with other words in order to facilitate learning and remembering them.

word class: see **part of speech**.

word field: see **lexical set**.

word formation: the creation of new words, for example by adding an **affix** (affixation) or constructing a **compound word**.

Further reading

Aitchison, J. 1987. *Words in the Mind: An Introduction to the Mental Lexicon*. Oxford: Basil Blackwell. A very accessible work by an expert in the field, full of insights into how we learn, store, and use vocabulary.

Carter, R. and **M. McCarthy.** 1988. *Vocabulary and Language Teaching*. Harlow: Longman. A very readable look at how words are learnt, with contributions by leading lights on new directions in vocabulary studies.

Applied Linguistics 2/3. 1981. A special issue on dictionaries, with contributions from a number of leading lights on different aspects of dictionaries.

Ellis, G. and **B. Sinclair.** 1989. *Learning to Learn English: A Course in Learner Training*. Cambridge: Cambridge University Press. One of the first books to address the issue of learning strategies and efficient learning.

Gairns, R. and **S. Redman.** 1986. *Working with Words: A Guide to Teaching and Learning Vocabulary*. Cambridge: Cambridge University Press. A practical book that introduces linguistic and psychological theories relevant to vocabulary learning, and has pages of ideas for lessons.

Hedge, T. 1988. *Writing*. Resource Books for Teachers series. Oxford: Oxford University Press. Contains many ideas for exploiting writing in class.

Ilson, R. (ed.) 1985. *ELT Documents 120: Dictionaries, Lexicography and Language Learning*. Oxford: Pergamon Press. A collection of interesting papers on different aspects of dictionaries, from research and practical classroom perspectives, with an excellent contribution from Adrian Underhill on working with learner's dictionaries.

Lakoff, R. and **M. Johnson.** 1980. *Metaphors We Live By*. Chicago: Chicago University Press. A classic study of the importance of metaphor, especially metaphorical fields, with hundreds of examples.

Lewis, M. 1993. *The Lexical Approach*. Hove: LTP.

Lewis, M. 1997. *Implementing the Lexical Approach*. Hove: LTP. Two books that explain the advantages of a lexical approach to learning and teaching, complete with practical examples of classroom activities.

McCarthy, M. 1990. *Vocabulary*. Language Teaching: A Scheme for Teacher Education series. Oxford: Oxford University Press.

Morgan, J. and **M. Rinvolucri.** 1986. *Vocabulary*. Resource Books for Teachers series. Oxford: Oxford University Press. Over a hundred classroom activities for teaching vocabulary in active and creative ways, including a section on games using dictionaries.

Ooi, D. and **J. L. Kim–Seoh.** 1996. 'Vocabulary teaching: looking behind the word.' *English Language Teaching Journal* 50/1: 52–8.

Redman, S. and **M. Ellis.** 1997. *A Way with Words: Resource Packs 1 & 2.* Cambridge: Cambridge University Press. Two photocopiable resource books full of worksheets to help students develop their vocabulary learning skills.

Rudzka, B. *et al.* 1981. *The Words You Need.* London: Macmillan.

Rudzka, B. *et al.* 1985. *More Words You Need.* London: Macmillan. Two coursebooks that contain a tremendous variety of vocabulary-learning activities.

Sinclair, J. 1991. *Corpus, Concordance, Collocation.* Oxford: Oxford University Press. A classic that explains the need for the vast database that underpins the Cobuild project, and insights that derived from establishing it.

Sheldon, L. (ed.) 1987. *ELT Document 126: ELT Textbooks and Materials: Problems in Evaluation and Development.* Modern English Publications.

Tickoo, M. L. (ed.) 1989. *Learners' Dictionaries: State of the Art.* Singapore: SEAMEO Regional Language Centre. A collection of papers on different aspects of dictionaries from theoretical, practical, and lexicographical perspectives.

Willis, D. 1990. *The Lexical Syllabus.* London: Collins Cobuild.

Other materials

Most learners' dictionaries are now published together with separate booklets of worksheets which act as guides to the dictionary itself, and which contain a number of helpful activities intended to offer students basic training in reading and understanding the dictionary. These are often free, and publishers are happy to provide copies for teachers and students. The materials are stimulating and are highly recommended. You might try the following:

Cambridge International Dictionary of English: Photocopiable Worksheets. ISBN 0 521 92762 5.

Learning Real English with Collins Cobuild English Language Dictionary. ISBN 0 003 70332 0.

Making the Most of Dictionaries in the Classroom: A Guide for Teachers of English. Oxford University Press. ISBN 0 19 470221 9.

Oxford Advanced Learner's Dictionary: Worksheets. ISBN 0 19 431103 1.

Oxford Elementary Learner's Dictionary: Worksheets. ISBN 0 19 470229 4.

Oxford Wordpower Dictionary: Free Worksheets. ISBN 0 19 431173 2.

Index

Other titles in the Resource Books for Teachers series